Aust
Gap
Pack

C000186206

First published in 2006 by Collins
an imprint of
HarperCollins Publishers
77–85 Fulham Palace Road
London
W6 8JB

The Collins website address is:
www.collins.co.uk

Created by Focus Publishing, Sevenoaks, Kent
Project editor: Guy Croton
Editor: Vanessa Townsend
Project designer: Neil Adams

Master designer: Laura Meseguer

ISBN-13   978-0-00-722896-6
ISBN-10   0-00-722896-1

Printed and bound in Great Britain by Clays Ltd, St Ives plc

Read this first!

Australia is one of the most popular tourist destinations on earth, and it can be an absolute paradise for those who want to turn their gap year into the working experience of a lifetime. The *Australia Gap Pack* has been created to provide you with all the information you need to turn your dream of a gap year 'Down Under' into an incredibly fulfilling reality, and consists of five main sections:

Section One shows you how using specialist companies can turn your working holiday into the trip of a lifetime. It covers all aspects of how you should set about getting work in Australia.

Section Two introduces you to the real nitty gritty of planning a working holiday Down Under. Whether you need information on insurance, booking accommodation, arranging your visa, getting your head around tax or sorting out a bank account, you'll find it all in our Travel Essentials section.

Section Three provides separate guides to the most popular city destinations among gap workers, namely: Sydney, Melbourne, Brisbane, Perth, Adelaide, Cairns, Darwin and Hobart. This section is indispensable for anyone needing to find work in these cities.

Section Four is a complete directory of websites that no self-respecting gap worker can afford to ignore. Use these information sites wisely and you will have access to all the knowledge you could ever need.

Section Five is a traveller's checklist. Use it more as a guideline rather than a 'take everything on it' list or you will end up paying vast amounts in excess baggage costs!

As you can see, no aspect of spending your gap year in Australia has been neglected. So sit down, put your feet up and get ready to start planning a working experience you will never forget.

Good luck!

Contents

Introduction

Welcome to *Australia Gap Pack*!

Planning a working holiday in any country can be challenging, and when that country just happens to be on the opposite side of the world, the prospect can often be very daunting. The *Australia Gap Pack* was created to help you research, plan and enjoy your gap year 'Down Under' with as little stress as possible. In essence, we have done much of the hard work for you. Our team of experienced travellers, backpackers and experts have combined their efforts to provide you with what we consider to be the most useful guide for gap year workers yet available.

This guide represents an evolutionary leap forward for us, because it not only builds on the success of our previous edition, but it also includes a great deal of additional information that has been suggested by our ongoing research and travelling experience.

The main destinations that are covered in this revised and expanded edition include Adelaide, Brisbane, Cairns, Canberra, Darwin, Hobart, Melbourne, Perth and Sydney. These are cities which the vast majority of working holidaymakers can rely on to help them make and spend their Australian dollars while having a barrel-load of fun at the same time. In this new edition we also include details of smaller and lesser known destinations that also provide good working opportunities for those who want something a bit different.

Throughout the guide we will introduce you to a number of companies that have a wealth of experience in assisting travellers like yourself. Think of these as our personal recommendations to help you obtain specific advice on getting a visa, exploring Australia or getting work in particular areas.

Right now you probably have a lot more questions than answers. You want to know how to work without breaking any laws, how to travel safely, where you'll be able to stay, how to find a job quickly, how much you can expect to earn and a whole lot more. All of these questions are perfectly natural, and by the time you have finished this guide you will have answers to each and every one of them.

So, relax. We've done all the tedious graft so that you won't have to! All you have to do is read on...

Travel safely

The British Foreign & Commonwealth Office has launched a campaign promoting safe travel. Go to: *www.fco.gov.uk/knowbeforeyougo* to check safety reports on countries, find out more about your destination and browse through their backpacker section.

o Darwin

NORTHERN
TERRITORY

Alice
o Springs

QUEENSLAND

WESTERN

AUSTRALIA

SOUTH
AUSTRALIA

o Brisbane

Kalgoorlie
o

Perth o

NEW SOUTH WALES

o Adelaide

o Sydney

VICTORIA
o
Melbourne

TASMANIA
Hobart o

_1 Working
in Australia

Thousands of backpackers head to Oz every year in search of sun, sea, sand and... work. Whether it's temporary work in an office or seasonal work picking fruit or shearing sheep on a farm in the Outback, there's a huge variety of jobs for you to choose from. However, it can be hard to know where to start, and that's where the *Australia Gap Pack* comes in! We've gathered together the most up-to-date information and tried to explain the options in the most straightforward way possible. The first part of the book is split into the following sections:

- **Sponsoring agencies**
- **Paid work**
- **Internships**
- **Placements**
- **Volunteering**
- **Visas**

Then, later on, we'll provide you with actual contacts within each city. We've focused on bar work, hotel work, office work and some language schools to get you started. Our listings provide all the information, names, addresses and contact details you need to help you to organize your working holiday in Australia.

Sponsoring agencies

Arriving in Australia without any definite plans can be quite daunting – especially when it is so far away from home and such a huge country. If you are a bit wary of going it alone, you may prefer to go on an organized working holiday in Oz. There are various organizations which provide such schemes and one of the best known ones is BUNAC's Work Australia programme.

BUNAC is a non-profit organization which arranges work and travel programmes for students and young people to various countries. The Work Australia programme allows participants to take any job, anywhere in Australia. The programme goes beyond the existing Australian Government Working Holidaymaker scheme by providing BUNAC's back-up help and support both before departure and throughout your stay, through BUNAC's subsidiary IEP. IEP takes care of you on arrival, providing support, accommodation during the early days and orientation, as well as job and travel hints, and 'on-the-spot' assistance when needed. The group flight departures also provide the ideal opportunity to meet with fellow participants.

For more info: *www.bunac.org*

Paid work

There is plenty of paid work for you in Australia once you get yourself legal. This part of *Australia Gap Pack* will take you through the options.

Office work

Note: The average adult weekly wage in Australia is around AUS $990. www.abs.gov.au

Working holidays in Oz don't have to mean glass collecting or fruit picking. If you have office skills, then use them! Bear in mind, however, that on a working holiday visa you can only work for three months with

EMMA YATES SPENT HER GAP YEAR AS A PARTICIPANT ON BUNAC'S WORK AUSTRALIA PROGRAMME.

'I set off on BUNAC's Work Australia programme with visions of a world of sun and surf. Australia was certainly this but also a whole lot more. The diversity and sheer vastness of this country is nothing less than incredible. My adventure began with 40 other BUNACers, eight of whom were to be my flatmates in Sydney for the following three months. After a few days, nine of us moved into a luxury apartment near Darling Harbour and by then I'd also found work as a waitress at the harbour. I spent the next nine months travelling through every state and territory, working to earn money as I went along. Some of my favourite memories are doing voluntary work out in the Australian bush of the Northern Territories in a place called Rum Jungle. I'd never pictured myself shovelling manure on an organic farm in the blistering heat, but watching the most amazing sunsets from our roof at the end of the day with a glass of ice cold beer in my hand more than made up for it! My other good memories were spotting my first kangaroo, going to an Aussie Rules football game, learning to surf and sleeping out in 'swags' under the stars... even though we did get rained on! In fact, no two days on the road were ever the same. From the exciting cities of Sydney and Melbourne, the rainforests and mountains of Tasmania and the deep red soil of the Australian outback – this certainly is a country where you can find it all.'

any one employer, so you are unlikely to appeal to many employers who would prefer to have long-term staff. For this reason temping agencies are your best bet. In all larger cities there is a well-established supply of, and demand for, temporary staff with working holiday visas.

If you're reading this book, it is likely you will have to work whilst you are overseas. Although there are more backpackers in Oz than ever before, and the economy has seen better times, experienced staff will always be required by good agencies.

A copy of your CV can be saved on your email. This means you can simply print it off when you need it, without getting it crumpled up in your backpack. Take a smart outfit for interviews and work, or you can always budget to buy a suit and some shoes when you are over there. Clothes tend to be cheaper in Australia than in the UK or Ireland.

At Christmas and New Year there are considerably less office temp opportunities throughout Australia. Offices close for the holidays and businesses are winding down. A better time of year is around May/June, when the tax year is ending and businesses are doing a lot of bookwork.

Office admin and secretarial

Office agencies are looking for people with the full range of secretarial and admin skills. If you know how to use Microsoft applications and have a typing speed of 55 wpm or over, then contact an employment agency. You can email your CV to one of the agencies in this book or give them a call when you arrive. In a secretarial/office support role you can expect to earn between AUS$16 to AUS$25 per hour, depending on your skills and the position.

IT and accounting

If you are a qualified accountant then you should not need to pick fruit or be a lap dancer on your travels (unless, of course, you want to!).

JOB AGENCIES

Make sure you check out the websites of some of Australia's top job agencies if you're looking for paid work:

HAYS – *www.hays.com.au/job/index.aspx*

HALLIS – *www.hallis.com.au*

EXACT RECRUITMENT – *www.exact.com.au*

INTEGRATED GROUP – *www.intgroup.com.au*

KELLY SERVICES – *kellyservices.com.au*

MOMENTUM CONSULTING – *www.momentumconsulting.com.au*

ROBERT WALTERS – *www.robertwalters.com*

Along with accountancy, IT is a sector where skilled people are in demand. Experience in programming languages, operating systems, databases and internet technologies are especially sought after.

Hospitality work

Working in bars, hotels, restaurants and resorts is an obvious way to earn money while in Australia. Hotel, tourism and leisure companies need most staff during school holidays, at Easter and Christmas. Resorts have the highest demand for staff in the summer, which is December to February. If you are looking for a solid three months of work, this can be a good opportunity to head to the Gold or Sunshine Coast. Think about the west coast if you are looking for resort work at this time of year. It has many beautiful resorts, and there isn't as much competition for work from other travellers.

Keeping your 'black and whites' at the ready is a sure way to impress catering agencies and restaurants. However, if you don't have room in your rucksack, or prefer not to have them screwed up, budget for a pair of tailored black trousers, a plain white shirt and some black shoes when you get to Australia. Black shoes should be plain, preferably lace ups, and should cover the whole of your foot (whatever you do, don't turn up in sandals!). Aussie bars and restaurants love experienced staff. The more bar and waiting experience you can get before you leave, the better.

If you have worked in an upmarket restaurant before, you stand more chance of getting work in a place with good tips in Oz. Beware though – tipping isn't as common in Australia as it is elsewhere.

'A la carte' experience is something that ads for waiting staff frequently require. It basically means you will be expected to show the customer to their table, hand out menus and take orders from the table. Silver service looks good on your CV, too.

If you can make a cappuccino or espresso using a proper coffee machine, you will be able to get a lot more work in cafes and bars.

The RSA (Responsible Serving of Alcohol) certificate is useful if you are planning on doing a lot of bar work. Hospitality agencies will charge you a fee to do your course, which takes around four hours to complete.

Many bars and restaurants require their staff to have this qualification, particularly in New South Wales.

If you have good references, bring them with you to show to employers. It could give you the edge over other applicants by having them to hand.

Each state has its own 'award rate' or minimum wage for work in the hospitality and catering sector.

Check out: *www.wagenet.gov.au* for up to date information on this. As a rough guide, however, you can expect to earn (per hour): Waiter – $14 to $21; Chef – $21 to $28; Kitchen hand – $13 to $20.

Nursing

There are two types of nurse in Australia:

- Registered nurse – university educated and qualified.
- Enrolled nurse – an enrolled nurse works under the supervision of a registered nurse.

The guidelines below apply to both types of nurse, so it needs to be done whichever side of the line you fall under.

To work as a nurse in Australia with a working holiday visa you should apply to the Nurse Regulatory Authority (NRA) in the state or territory in which you wish to work. You should do this before you arrive in Australia.

Nurses have to be registered in the state they wish to practise in. The NRA of your chosen territory will check that you can demonstrate that you meet the national nursing competency standards. These are required for all territories.

Some nationalities have to do a 'competency based assessment program' when they arrive in Oz. If you are from the UK, Ireland or Canada, you don't have to. If you are not on a Working Holiday Makers (WHM) visa (see pages 35–7), you will have to go through the Australian Nursing Council (ANCI) to complete an assessment. WHM visa holders do not have to do this, but ANCI recommend that you

NURSING JOB AGENCIES

Make sure you check out the websites of some of the top agencies in Australia if you're looking for nursing work:

ALLIANCE HEALTH SERVICES – *www.alliancehealth.com.au*

NURSING EXCELLENCE – *www.nursexel.com.au*

OBS HEALTH – *www.OBSHealth.com*

MEDISTAFF – *www.medistaff.com.au*

do as it can save you time (apparently) when you try to register with the state Nurses Regulatory Authority. If you have registered with the NRA in Queensland for example, you can work in other states as they have a mutual recognition of registration.

For more information, look at the following websites:

Australian Nursing and Midwifery Council – *www.anmc.org.au*

Visa regulations for nurses – *www.immi.gov.au/migration/nurses.htm*

Teaching

The federal system in Australia means that each state and territory has different rules and regulations for registering overseas qualified teachers.

The schools system in Australia has three basic levels:

- pre-school education
- primary education
- secondary education

Pre-school education is not compulsory and ranges from part time to full time, depending on which state you are in.

Children start primary education at 5 or 6 years old, again depending on state legislation. The primary school curriculum includes English, maths, science, history, geography, technology, arts and PE. It is not uncommon for a primary school to teach a second language as well as English. One class teacher teaches most major subjects and stays with the class throughout the day.

A child's attendance at secondary school is compulsory until they are 15 or 16, depending on state or territory legislation. Secondary school teachers should be able to teach at least two subjects to a high level. An Australian teacher will have done at least four years' full time study. This will include a minimum of six weeks full time supervised teaching practice.

Australian secondary schools are mostly comprehensive high schools. The last two years of secondary education may be taught in specialist colleges. Apart from state schools, there are also many Catholic, charitably funded and independent schools in Australia. In line with the size and variety of the country, the range of schools goes from large urban schools to one-teacher outlets in tiny rural towns.

As someone on a working holiday visa you will be eligible to apply to teach on a casual status. You will need to obtain a Casual Approved Number from the department of education in the state you want to work in – bear in mind this can take a few weeks. You will also need a full transcript of all the courses and your university qualifications, including your degree and/or diploma certificates. Casual supply teachers are often thrown in at the deep end – you could be working in particularly poor or run down schools where the usual teachers are often on leave. Prepare yourself for this aspect of the work. Areas where there are particular shortages of teachers include maths, science and languages.

You must register as a teacher before you can begin work. In Queensland and Southern Australia, all teachers must be registered. The Registered Schools Board must register all teachers in non-government schools in Victoria. In New South Wales and Western Australia your eligibility to teach is determined by the relevant Department of Education for government schools. Non-government schools are able to decide for themselves who they will employ.

If you are on a working holiday visa, you must contact the relevant authority to establish your credentials and make sure your experience matches the state requirements. See the city teaching pages of the Pack for contact details of State Educational Departments.

Harvest work

Australia has a huge farming industry and fruit picking is a tried and tested form of backpacker graft. It can be hard work, and it won't make you rich, but fruit picking is a good way to see other bits of the country and meet people. One of the reasons that the Australian government is so keen to set up working holiday programmes with other countries is that there is a chronic shortage of workers to help with harvesting.

Harvesting can involve a lot of different tasks – everything from fruit picking to driving the tractors or feeding the workers. You name it, Australia grows it. Apricots, asparagus, melons, bananas – you could pick them all.

Fruit picking is often a fall back option for backpackers in need of some quick cash. The picking season or harvest generally climaxes during the Australian summer, but although most fruit such as grapes, plums and mangos ripen between December and May, there are still picking opportunities to be had all year round. This is because it isn't just fresh fruit being harvested; prawns, lobsters and tobacco also need to be harvested.

It isn't a laid back lifestyle though, as you will have to put in some hard work. You will start around 4am and finish just as the sun is

Some things you need to remember to take:
- Sun cream, a good pair of shades with UV protective lenses and a protective hat.
- A hardy pair of gloves to offer protection from thistles, thorns and biting insects.
- Plenty of water. Drink often to avoid dehydration and heat sickness.
- Protective and comfortable footwear – preferably boots which will protect ankles from snakes and pest control chemicals.
- Insect repellent.
- Cash to tide you over in case the weather puts back the harvest.

becoming it's angriest around midday. Consequently, physical fitness and stamina are definitely useful attributes.

The payment will either be per hour, where anything upward of $10 an hour is a good wage, or by the bucket. Hourly rates are usually for picking grapes in the vineyards, as they have to be in pristine condition. So it's all about quality, not quantity. Being paid per bucket is usually the norm though, so the more effort you put in, the more money you'll make. It's not uncommon for food and accommodation to be paid for, but obviously these vary from farm to farm.

A point to remember:
It's best to be relatively fit as harvesting is tiring work with long hours!

For more info:
www.jobsearch.gov.au/harvesttrail/
www.anyworkanywhere.com
www.pickingjobs.com
Employment National: call 13 34 44 (This number will only work when dialled in Australia)

CASE STUDY

MILDURA IS IN NORTH WESTERN VICTORIA AND IS KNOWN AS THE 'GATEWAY TO THE OUTBACK'.

Between February and April there is lots of work and they encourage travellers with working holiday visas to come along. (You could be earning $13 to $15 per hour for vineyard work, up to seven days a week.) Some growers provide huts for pickers to sleep and cook in, but if you have a tent you will be at an advantage as accommodation is limited. You will often be working in temperatures of around 20-35 degrees, with an early start to avoid the worst of the afternoon sun. Expect to be paid one week after you start.

Ski work

Ski work in Australia? Surely not! Well, there are plenty of ski resorts in Australia that are looking for workers over the winter season.

New South Wales and Victoria have got the majority of the ski resorts in Australia, and it's here that many people head, looking for ski work. It's also worth checking out Tasmania. Although the resorts are smaller and the snow is less reliable, it's well worth having a look as Tasmania is one of the most stunning destinations on the planet.

It's definitely cheaper to ski in Australia, although the resorts are smaller. Because they are smaller there are less jobs around, but with a bit of persistence you should be able to find something. The Australian winter is our summer, with the season running from June through to October.

The kind of jobs available during the ski season include lift operators, janitors, bar and restaurant staff, guest services, equipment rental and repair, day care, ticket checking, parking attendants, cashiers, retail staff, room attendants and, of course, ski and snowboard instructors.

Most positions require you to have some experience in the relevant field, whether it's just customer services or catering. If you want to work as a ski or snowboard instructor, you will need to have the relevant qualifications.

The largest ski resorts are the places where you are most likely to find work. As an employee of one of the big resorts you can expect to have low pay and shared accommodation. However, you can also expect a discount on ski passes, subsidized accommodation and food, as well as an active social life! So if you are there for the love of the snow, rather than the need to earn lots of money, you'll be fine.

BUNAC placements allow you to pretty much choose the kind of work you want to do. BUNAC suggests that you work for more than one employer at the same time – just don't stay in the same job for more than three months.

Many people who go on a BUNAC placement sort out their work before they go – and that could be a job in one of Australia's ski resorts.

For more info: *www.bunac.org*

Internships

An internship (the Australian word for a work experience placement) is a great opportunity for you to use your gap year to build on your skills and experience in a way that will be vitally useful when you finish your formal education and enter the world of work. Employers are no longer impressed by people who say they have just been 'travelling' in their gap year. Doing an internship will show them that you're skilled, experienced and mature enough to cope in a business environment.

The best way to organize a work placement is to arrange it through an organization like those listed below in this section. They'll support you from application through to the end of your placement, which can make things a lot easier. It can be a daunting experience – starting a new job is stressful enough, so imagine doing it in another country! They'll place you with companies that match your requirements and ensure that you are looked after every step of the way throughout your placement.

You'll most probably be placed with other interns, so you won't feel completely on your own, and you'll work in a company in an industry that is matched to your academic or professional development. This means that if you want to be a radio presenter and you're planning to study journalism at university, then you could spend time at an Australian radio station learning the ropes. The focus is very much on industry training and on helping to prepare you for your professional life.

One great internship organization is **Australian Internships**. They will give you a fantastic chance to train in Australia with a variety of businesses across a broad range of industries. Some of Australia's top companies offer internships, and you can choose anything from Accounting to Media and Journalism, Forestry to Graphic Design.

Find out more at *www.internships.com.au*

Another company worth checking out is **ISPC** – they pick you up from the airport, and look after you all the way. They offer professional, hospitality and rural placements.

Find out more at *www.ispc.com.au*

Global Choices also run internships Down Under, placing you with some of the top companies in Oz and providing you with plenty of support from beginning to end.

Find out more at *www.globalchoices.co.uk*

Volunteering

Voluntary placements, eco-tourism, community development projects, treks and expeditions all offer pure adventure and an incredible experience which can be part or all of your gap year. It all costs, but the returns are huge – and many of the organizations who provide placements will also give you help and advice on raising the money to pay for it. This can be as valuable as the experience itself, as it shows that you can motivate yourself and, more importantly, motivate other people to give you money. This impresses business people, and will put you in a great position when you try and get a job!

Some of you will have dreams of doing something for the world. Maybe you look at politicians and think 'I could do better than that' – and maybe you can. The problem is that it's tricky to do it on your own. However, there are plenty of companies who share your vision and who would love you to help them out.

You'll spend your time with a group of people just as dedicated as you – so you'll meet people, do something you believe in, help the natural world, travel, learn new skills and give yourself the confidence that will help you in the future. Need any more reasons?

Organizations that run voluntary placements
There are plenty of companies who are looking for volunteers to work on their projects – the problem is which one to choose! Here's a quick guide to the companies and charitable organizations who are looking for volunteers to work Down Under:

BUNAC

A BUNAC working holiday abroad can give you the opportunity to develop new skills, gain independence, meet new people, earn money and experience adventure! Australia is an incredible country in which to spend a working holiday, and going with BUNAC can make the whole process a lot easier.

You can stay for up to a year in Australia with BUNAC, working and travelling as you go. BUNAC's subsidiary organization, IEP (International Exchange Programs), will help you to find work and accommodation.

BUNAC is a non-profit, member club which has been offering work and travel programmes abroad for students and other young people for over 42 years.

For more info: *www.bunac.org.uk/uk/workaustralia*

Global Adventures

Global Adventures is an exciting Gap Year programme that allows you to design your own truly unique year abroad. For a one-off fee, you get a round-the-world ticket with up to six or ten stops and the opportunity to join up to four of their eight core programmes in the USA, Brazil, Europe, South Africa, India, Borneo, Belize and Guatemala and Australia/New Zealand, with plenty of time for independent travel in between.

Help with arranging your flight ticket is only just the start. Before you leave, you'll be invited to a one to one consultation session to help you select the right core programmes, and an intensive two-day pre-departure orientation course with all the information and travel tips you need to know in order to be fully prepared for your adventure of a lifetime. And while you're away, you'll travel safe in the knowledge that you're fully covered by Global Adventures' network of local agents – so wherever you are in the world, there's always someone to turn to for help and guidance if you need it.

For more info: *www.globaladventures.co.uk*

Work and Travel Co

Work and Travel Company will help you, well, work and travel! They have a selection of fantastic packages designed purely for people who want to work and travel or who want to volunteer. You can get paid work or volunteer on conservation projects in Australia. They'll help you to organize your gap year, whether you want a paid job on a ranch in the Outback or volunteer work helping Australia's unique environment.

For more info: *www.worktravelcompany.co.uk*

GAP Activity Projects

GAP Activity Projects are the biggest volunteer year out organization for school-leavers in the UK. They were established in 1972 and send up to 2,000 young people from the UK to 32 countries (including Australia) each year on structured work placements.

Volunteers, aged between 17 and 25, can get involved in a variety of projects, including teaching English, classroom assistance, caring, conservation, outdoor and medical work.

For more info: *www.gap.org.uk*

i-to-i

i-to-i is a leading travel and TEFL (Teaching English as a Foreign Language) training organization. The company offers around 300 different volunteer projects in 24 countries, to people of all ages. It also specializes in short TEFL courses, available either online or over a single weekend, in locations throughout the UK, Ireland and Australia.

For more info: *www.i-to-i.com*

Overseas Working Holidays

Overseas Working Holidays offer Working Holiday packages to Australia – from jobs at the Melbourne Spring racing Carnival to work at the Australian Grand Prix. They will also find you hospitality work throughout the year.

Their aim is to take the hassle out of working holidays provide jobs, bank accounts, tax file numbers and accommodation if required.

For more info: *www.overseasworkingholidays.co.uk*

Fundraising

Many of the organizations that people volunteer with on their gap years are charities. The work they do can range from sustainable development projects to conservation to community health initiatives. Because they are charities, the money that you pay to go with them is often in the form of a donation (they'll suggest the minimum amount they require), and it's up to you to raise the money in any way you fancy. This means that the work you do for them and the money that you pay is all going towards fulfilling the aims of charity.

You could get sponsorship from a local company, from your old school or from family and friends – the main thing is that the fundraising is in some ways almost as important as the volunteering itself. Not only are you giving money to a good cause, but you are also proving to yourself and other people that you can be persuasive, persistent and single-minded when you get your teeth into something that is important to you... and it looks great on your CV! Employers will be very impressed if you can prove that you have experience of getting other people to part with their cash for something you believe in. Anything you can do to set yourself apart from the crowd will do your job prospects a lot of good.

Sporting gap years

Are you good at sports? Do you fancy getting better? Aussies are renowned for being sports-mad and for their action-packed approach to life. Every imaginable activity is on offer – from extreme sports like bungee-jumping and sky-diving to more traditional pursuits such as cricket. Many travellers will include these sports on their already jam-packed itineraries, but these activities can now form the basis of your ultimate year out!

What can I do?

A number of companies offer the chance to live, train and play sport all over Oz, becoming fully-fledged members of their designated clubs for a full season and combining a passion for sport with exciting, independent travel opportunities. They offer placements playing all kinds of sports, including cricket, hockey, rugby, netball and football, in clubs all over the country. Participants are usually located in lively, vibrant cities such as Sydney, Melbourne, Perth and Brisbane, but most companies are continually expanding their selection of sports and adding exciting new locations for gappers to fall in love with. A fulfilling gap year is guaranteed as participants experience a side of Australia that most travellers will never get to see.

What's in it for me?

Much of the focus is on playing rather than coaching sport, although there are often opportunities to get involved with junior activities or teams that may also form part of your designated club, allowing you to give something back to the community that has supported you during your stay, while boosting those invaluable interpersonal training skills. A sporting placement can seriously boost your personal development - your CV will look highly attractive to any future potential employers, with a sports placement that demonstrates great commitment, team-work and leadership skills combined with a structured gap year that takes confidence, independence and self motivation, ensuring you get the advantage in any career path you choose to take. Developing your game, having loads of fun, making loads of new friends and experiencing all the best that Australia has to offer are just some of the things you can expect to love about a year away playing sport.

Why should I do it?

Well, first of all, if you're already good at sports, you want to get better at sports or you just love sport, this is a great way to spend part or all of your gap year. A sporting gap year is also valuable in a number of other ways:

Help other people through sport!

If you've got a talent for a particular sport, then maybe you've also got a talent for teaching other people, and for helping them to improve their quality of life through sport. You can pass on some of your knowledge and passion for sport and use it as an opportunity to genuinely help people in other areas of their lives – helping them to build confidence, improve their English or just to stay healthy and happy. And if you really put the effort in, you'll also come out of the experience with new skills and new self-confidence of your own.

Including sport in your gap year is a great way to have fun, do something you really enjoy, help other people and even improve your own skills. It can give you confidence and new qualifications that can change your life. Just ask yourself this – if you're a good footballer, why spend your time doing a tedious job when you could be earning money teaching other people to play better? Use your talents and get formal recognition for them so that you can ultimately make some money out of them – and help other people in the process. Whether you're into rugby, football or cricket, winter sports like skiing and snowboarding, or water sports like scuba diving, if you reckon you've got skills that you could share with other people, then use your gap year to get professional recognition for them. If you're at a very basic level or a complete novice, many sporty gap years focus on playing rather than coaching.

Get a sporting qualification!

Every activity in your gap year should build your skills and experience in a practical way. Once you head to uni or to work you should be able to do more than you did when you left school – and earning a sporting qualification is a great addition to your CV. It is also something that is potentially life-changing, if it means that you can dedicate your career to teaching other people to play the sport you love and get paid for it.

Once you've finished your training you'll be a qualified coach or instructor, and can then look for work anywhere in the world! So what kind of qualifications are available? Well, that depends on what your level is and what you want to do with your qualifications once you've got them. Some courses are for people at a basic level, others require you to have a minimum level of ability. As with any kind of qualification, make sure you know whether the certificate is internationally recognized. There's not much point in working hard for a diving certificate or a football coaching qualification if the piece of paper they give you at the end is worth nothing.

Resort work

Not everybody wants to be a professional in a particular sport – maybe you've done it a few times on holiday and just want to get more experience. One great way to do just that is to live and work at a resort. Whether it's a ski resort in the Snowy Mountains or a resort on the Gold Coast where you can spend your free time learning to surf, it can be a great way to spend more time with the sport you love. You could be serving drinks, waiting on tables, slaving away in a hotel kitchen or working as a rep for a tour company – whatever you do the chances are that the perks will be fantastic. When you're not working you can train in your chosen sport, and when you're not doing that you'll be socializing!

What about the beach?

Oz is famous for its beaches and water sports – diving, surfing, yachting, sailing and windsurfing are some of the activities that are also on offer, whether you just want to train up or become a fully qualified instructor. One of the most popular programmes bases you in Sydney, living in the seaside suburb of Manly, with its upbeat holiday resort atmosphere, only ten minutes by JetCat from the heart of the city itself. You'll live in apartments located right on the famous beach front; with its fabulous golden sands home to numerous beach volleyball and surf competitions! Elsewhere, there are also opportunities for Professional Dive Training and International Yacht Training on the Great Barrier Reef.

Worried about cash?

Some companies also offer the chance to work during the days you are not training or playing with your club in Australia; this not only provides you with that all-important extra cash, but excellent work experience as well. Other companies will train you to become an instructor for your chosen sport, allowing you to earn money doing what you love after you have completed your qualification.

Australia is a big favourite with sports fans from all over the globe, with its diverse environment enabling it to become home to a huge variety of weird and wonderful sporting activities. As well as the sport-crazy, get-up-and-go atmosphere, the beach-bums, the bush walking and, of course, the BBQs have all become defining symbols of that laid-back Aussie lifestyle that is renowned all over the world. Participating in a sport-based gap provides you with a real sense of Australia that so many travellers will never get to experience. If it's a true taste of life in the land Down Under that you're after, then a sport-based gap year provides you with an unmissable opportunity to throw caution to the wind and, in true Aussie action-style, leap head first into the experience of a lifetime – you certainly won't regret it!

Sport Lived are a gap year company that arrange for people like you to play sport in Oz. Their mission is to provide safe, well organized and constructive gap years for people with a love of sport. They cater for a range of ages and abilities and aim to create a gap year that is individually tailored to your requirements. This means finding a suitable sports club which matches your ability and arranging accommodation with other people who share your passion for sport.

For more info visit: *www.gapwork.com* and *www.sportlived.co.uk*.

Major sporting events jobs

With the Aussies' love of sport, the major sporting events throughout the year are a great chance to catch some fantastic action. They also provide a great opportunity to get work. From catering to waiting tables, bar work to stewarding, many companies are looking for extra staff during these busy times. Check out this list of some of the biggest sporting events happening Down Under and see if you can help out – it will be an unforgettable experience!

Major events

The 'Aussie Rules' league runs from March to September, culminating in the Grand Final to win the coveted AFL flag. The Victoria based teams are traditionally expected to claim the flag as a matter of course. Various venues.

For more info: *www.afl.com.au*

The AFL runs the State of Origin series, where the teams are picked based on where you were born. This runs through the end of June and the beginning of July. As Rugby is a winter sport, it runs from mid March to the end of September. Held at various venues.

For more info: *www.stateoforigin.com.au*

The Rugby League Tri-Nations is predominately held in the UK, but Australia and New Zealand play each other in their own country before flying over to play Great Britain starting around the middle of October.

For more info: *www.australianrugbyleague.com.au*

The cricketing spectacle of England versus Australia, otherwise known as the Ashes, is held every other year. As the last Ashes series was played in the summer of 2005 in England, the next battle will be during the winter of 2006/7 in Australia.

For more info: *www.cricket.com.au*

The Australian Golf Open is usually held at the end of November over four days.
For more info: *www.australianopengolf.com*

The Australian Tennis Open (one of the four Grand Slams) is played at Melbourne Park, Melbourne in January.
For more info: *www.australianopen.com*

The Adelaide International Horse Trials and Trans Tasman Championship, one of only four events of its calibre is held annually in the middle of November.
For more info: *www.adelaidehorsetrials.com.au*

The Australian Grand Prix is held in Melbourne and has been the season opener for nine years. It is usually at the beginning of March, but in 2006 was put back to 2 April, due to the Commonwealth Games in the city from 15–26 March.
For more info: *http://cars.grandprix.com.au*

The new Hyundai A-League football league began in 2005. The season runs from the end of August to February. Adelaide, Sydney and Melbourne are the cities where the main rivalries are, and with attendances becoming larger by the game, you can really revel in the atmosphere.
For more info: *www.a-league.com.au*

The Melbourne Cup – Australia's biggest horse race – is held on the first Tuesday in November in Melbourne.
For more info: *www.melbourneracingclub.net.au*

The Adelaide Cup Carnival is held for a fortnight each year in March and is the South Australian pinnacle of thoroughbred horse racing.
For more info: *www.sajc.com.au*

TIP

► Go to *www.whatsonwhen.com* to research all kinds of events throughout Australia.

► You can also access a full calendar of upcoming sporting events from the Australian Sports Commission web site at *www.ausport.gov.au*

Studying

Fancy studying in Oz as part of your gap year? Australia offers plenty of opportunities for anybody looking to add to their education and skills. Each year, hundreds of British students head to Australia to study or train, as well as to work and travel. Some people do their whole undergraduate or postgraduate degree at an Australian university; others enrol for just a semester or two. Others are looking for vocational training in a skill or profession, and some just want to do a short course or an internship as part of their gap year. There are loads of reasons for wanting to study in Australia – obviously starting with the very tempting opportunity it gives you to live in and travel around an incredibly beautiful, exciting country that enjoys a free, laid-back lifestyle at the same time as getting a world-class education. But, apart from that, there are a few other things that make studying in Australia a very attractive prospect.

Firstly, Australian universities offer plenty of places on courses that are so popular they're almost impossible to get into in the UK, such as dentistry, medicine, veterinary science and physiotherapy. There are also certain areas in which Australia is widely acknowledged as an academic world leader, and in which it offers unbeatable opportunities for practical experience. For example, if you were thinking of studying marine biology, where would you rather do it – in the English Channel or off the Great Barrier Reef? There's a massive range of subjects available in Australia – between all the universities as well as the numerous colleges, pretty much everything is offered somewhere. You can choose from a huge range, from traditional academic subjects like science, languages and the arts (these are usually offered by universities) to more vocational courses, like business, hospitality, tourism and sport, which are often specialities of the TAFEs or colleges.

The Australian education system is based on the British, so it's easy for UK students to fit in. The similarities between the two systems allows British students a lot of flexibility and choice – for example, some choose to study in Australia as part of a UK degree. Under university study abroad schemes, it's possible to get academic credit for overseas study, which then counts toward your degree at your home university. Academic standards are high, particularly in the universities. Australian universities have an international reputation for excellence in lots of different fields and are known for their innovative, research-intensive culture. In the *World University Rankings 2004*, published by *The Times Higher Education Supplement*, six Australian universities appeared in the top 50 – only eight UK institutions made that level of the list. Qualifications awarded by Australian universities are internationally recognized and highly regarded by employers and overseas universities alike.

Visas

The type of visa you'll need to study in Australia will be determined by how long your course is. If it is three months or less, you'll be able to enter Australia and study on a Tourist or Working Holiday Maker visa. All British citizens are eligible for a Tourist (short stay) visa – it entitles you to be in the country for up to three months, but not to undertake any form of paid work. If your course is longer than three months, you'll need to get a student visa. A student visa entitles you to be in the country for as long as your course lasts, and usually allows some time for travelling around, too. If your course is longer than a year, the conditions of your student visa will also allow you to work part-time for up to 20 hours a week while you are studying and for as many hours as you wish during your holidays. (You will need to make an application for your entitlement to work after you have commenced your course.) In order to apply for a student visa, you'll need to have an offer of study from your chosen institution.

Studying in Oz is a great gap year option – it gives you the chance to add to your skills, experience and qualifications while living in one of the most exciting places on the planet.

Study Options

Study Options is a unique independent education agency that helps students from the UK and Ireland choose and apply to their dream undergraduate degree, postgraduate degree, gap year course or internship in Australia or New Zealand. They will guide you through all the paperwork and planning involved with university applications – identifying which documents you need to provide, how they need to be verified, checking your university applications etc. They'll also let you know how far in advance you need to apply for your course, and when to put in your visa application.

Applications sent via Study Options are fast-tracked through their assessment procedures. They will do the worrying, the chasing and the sorting of paperwork for you, so that the experience of applying to study overseas is as stress-free as possible. And, best of all, their advice and services are absolutely free. They don't charge you for anything, no matter how many times you phone or email them with questions.

Want to know more? Get in touch with *www.studyoptions.com*

Working Holiday Makers visa

To work in Australia you need to apply for a Working Holiday Makers (WHM) visa. This cannot be granted in Australia but certain nationalities (including British people) may apply in any country except Australia.

▶ *Citizens of the following countries can obtain a Working Holiday Makers (WHM) visa for Australia in the UK: Canada, Denmark, Finland, Ireland, the Netherlands, Sweden, Norway and the UK.*

You have a year from the date your visa is issued in which to travel to Australia and you are allowed to stay in Australia for 12 months from the date you enter. You can travel in and out of Australia as many times as you like during the 12 months from the date of first entry. However, if you depart Australia during your 12 months stay you cannot 'top up' or recover the period of time spent outside the country.

▶ *From 1 November 2005 it became possible to apply for a second WHM visa, which will give you 12 more months in Oz. However, to be eligible you must spend three months under your first visa doing harvest work in one of the specified regions of the country. Go to* http://www.immi.gov.au/ allforms/visiting_whm.htm *for more details. The reason that the Australian government is so keen to get working holiday makers to stick around, is that the farms struggle to find enough workers during harvest time. Some are very remote and as there are far fewer people per square mile in Australia than there are in the UK, they value all the harvest workers they can get!*

The work restrictions on the visa mean you can only work for three months with any one employer, however there are no restrictions on the type of work you can do. A WHM visa also allows you to study or do training in Australia for up to three months as part of your year there.

A WHM visa is the best way of working legally and getting paid properly on your travels. If you are doing a round the world trip, Australia and New Zealand will be your likely port of calls for holiday and work. There are a number of criteria you must fulfil as a working holiday visa applicant for Australia:

Working Holiday Makers visa conditions
- Aged between 18-30 years.
- Not accompanied by dependent children.
- Show your main reason for coming to Australia is to holiday and any work you do is just to support yourself while in Australia.

- Have not previously entered Australia on a WHM visa (unless you have been a harvest worker – see previous page).
- Meet health and character requirements.
- Have funds of AUS$5,000 (approx £2,000).
- Upon arrival be able to provide an outward ticket or sufficient funds for one.

Processing your Australian WHM visa

You can only process your WHM visa online on the Australian Immigration website – www.immi.gov.au. If you would like assistance, then Travellers Contact Point provide a visa processing service for the e-visa for only £15 plus the embassy fee, which is currently AUS$170 (roughly £70). The Australian High Commission in London DOES NOT offer a mail, fax, telephone or public counter WHM visa service. You should receive a reply on the outcome of your visa within two working days. You don't have to send your passport, bank statement or any proof of funds. On arrival in Australia you have to go into the local DIMIA (Department of Immigration and Multicultural and Indigenous Affairs) office to get your passport stamped with your WHM visa. Embassy fees and processing methods can change at any time – for up to date information on the WHM visa, log on to *www.travellers.com.au* and click on 'Visas'.

Other types of visa

ETA (Electronic Travel Authority)

All travellers to Australia (apart from NZ citizens) require a visa. An ETA is issued electronically and is valid for 12 months allowing you to stay up to three months at a time in Australia. You can get an ETA from the Australian Embassy by applying online (for a charge of AUS$20) and travel agents (the cost will vary from £10–£14). Travellers Contact Point provides a quick and easy service for £10; just call with your passport details. It is strictly against the law to work on a visitor visa in Australia – with two exceptions: WWOOFing (Willing Workers On Organic Farms) and conservation work. Illegal labour is a political hot topic in Australia and the Department of Immigration will be only too happy to add you to the statistics of illegal workers they have caught and deported!

Tourist visitor visas

This visa does not allow you to work but you can visit Australia for up to six months. You are required to show that you are able to support yourself financially and it is open to any age group. The embassy charge is currently £30. To download the Application Form 48, log on to *www.travellers.com.au* and click on 'Visas'.

Student visa

The Australian government operates an Overseas Student Program (OSP) that allows people who are not Australian citizens to study in Australia. You must obtain a student visa (Form 157A) before you can begin a course of study in Australia. You can be granted a student visa

---

VISA INFORMATION

Travellers Contact Point website – *www.travellers.com.au*
enquiries@travellersuk.com
020 7243 7887

....

UK Australian Embassy: Migration Branch
Australian High Commission, Strand, London, WC2B 4LA
020 7379 4334, Mon-Fri 9am-11am
www.immi.gov.au

....

Australian Immigration and Citizenship Information Line
09065 508 900 (calls cost £1 per min)

TOP TIPS
▶ Try not to plan to get the job of your dreams on a working holiday visa but remember that any job done will add to your list of key skills. Make the best of what you are doing.
▶ Backpackers wanting to extend their visa for two years must have completed three months of seasonal harvest work at a regional farm in Australia. To find out where the seasonal work is, try *www.jobsearch.gov.au/harvesttrail.*
▶ Prepare your CV before you go and keep it on file on your email. Remember to bring references too.
▶ The Australian Yellow Pages is a great source of potential employers. Type in the business or sector you want to work in and get hunting! Go to *www.yellowpages.com.au*

only if you wish to undertake a registered course or part of a registered course on a full-time basis. Students on this scheme can work up to 20 hours per week and up to 40 hours during school holidays (around 12 weeks' school holidays per year). Travellers Contact Point represents several approved colleges and universities in and around Sydney. The Student Visa scheme is a great alternative to the working holiday for those of you torn between taking a 'gap year' and continuing with your studies. It is also suitable for those of you who have already used the WHM visa to return for another extended stay, and a good opportunity if you're looking to migrate. Studying in Australia and getting a qualification there can boost your migration points by up to 65 (110 points is required to be eligible to apply for migration).

Other visas such as those enabling permanent immigration, temporary employment or business in Australia are much harder to get than the tourist or working holiday visa. Getting one involves a lot of paperwork, time and effort with potential employers and lawyers. If you are eligible, a working holiday visa is by far the easiest way to work legally in Australia while travelling.

WORKING AUSTRALIA – LIVE FROM DOWN UNDER!

We came out to Australia two months ago with a Working Holiday Makers (WHM) visa. It was relatively easy to obtain our visas but we needed to plan quite well in advance, which I'm usually not very good at doing!

We arrived in Sydney and spent a few days adjusting to the time difference and getting ourselves familiar with the area – including the local bars! We stayed in backpacker accommodation for the first two weeks and managed to find a nice six month lease on the outskirts of the city.

I was planning to try and use the visa to get a really good job in business and my friend wanted to work in a gym. This is proving quite difficult to do! So we are both working as general admin staff in the city at the moment but it is great fun and pays the bills. We are also making good contacts for further work.

Bar and hotel work is pretty easy to get out here but we are trying not to do that if possible. The hours are long and hard and often unsocial. I'm afraid we want to play hard too!

I would advise others to sign up to an agency and also just to walk round and hand in your CV at companies you would like to work at. My friend is spending some time locating all the gyms in the area and visiting them. It pays to visit someone rather than just talk over the telephone.

Later on this year, we plan to work our way up the coast. We don't really mind what we do. We have found out about being able to extend our visa for another year if we get our hands dirty with some harvest work, so we are looking into that as we love it out here.

Income Tax

It may seem harsh as a humble traveller, but you will have to pay tax on any earnings while you are in Oz. In order to make sure you are paying the right amount of tax, you should have a tax file number (TFN). When you have your working holiday visa, and an address in Australia that the tax office can send your TFN to, you can apply online for a TFN – log on to *www.ato.gov.au/individuals*. However, you can only apply online for a TFN once you are in Australia. Once you have applied, it takes up to 28 days for the tax office to process your application.

Alternatively, you can call 13 28 61 when you arrive in Australia and make an appointment to apply in person at the following tax offices (don't forget your passport as ID):

Sydney Tax Office – 100 Market Street
Brisbane Tax Office – 280 Adelaide Street
Melbourne Tax Office – Casseldon Place 2 Lonsdale Street

If you have worked without a tax number, and have been paying a higher rate of tax, you could be entitled to a refund. Go to *www.ato.gov.au* to find out more about refunds and tax in general. Remember to keep payslips and your tax file number safe, in case you need to apply for a refund. If you can, get a Group Certificate from your employer before you leave. You need to hand in a written request at least 14 days before you finish work. Your Group Certificate is a record of all the tax you have paid in total during that period.

Remember:

* Keep all your pay slips.
* Get a copy of your final wage statement.

Goods and Services Tax (GST)

GST is charged at 10% on loads of things you will buy during your time in Oz. There is a tourist refund scheme, which means you can claim the tax back from any purchases over AUS$300 when you are at the airport on the way home. You will need all your receipts, and restrictions may apply. One restriction is that you can only claim the tax back on something you have bought up to 30 days before your departure date. Not much use if you have been travelling for a while!

Working in Australia
Frequently asked questions

► **Do I need a student ID card?**

Having proof of your status as a student is always a good idea, and we therefore recommend that you obtain a student ID card which is recognized wherever you go. The International Student Identity Card (ISIC) is the only student identity card which is recognized internationally, and is available to anyone aged 12 or over who is in full-time education. ID cards are also available for non-student travellers under the age of 26, and for full-time teachers and professors.

To find out more, visit *www.isic.org*

► **How do I prepare a good CV?**

Having a good CV will put you head and shoulders above the rest when it comes to landing a job. It is best to prepare the document on a computer using a standard template and to print out several copies. An Australian CV (or resumé as its also known Down Under) is much the same as its British counterpart, but you can find a good Aussie template on *www.mycareer.com.au*.

It stands to reason that you probably won't need a CV for fruit-picking, but for most other work, including bar work and temping, a CV is a must. A temping agency will look for a higher standard of CV than a bar manager, but as long as you emphasise your transferable skills, such as team work, communication, numeracy and ability to work on your own initiative, your CV should be relevant for most employers.

Send yourself a copy of your CV by email so that you can access it whilst abroad and print out extra copies as you need them. When writing the CV, aim to sell yourself, but don't go overboard on unnecessary details. A good CV should be no more than two A4 pages in length, and waffling on about your accomplishments is just as bad as saying nothing.

► **What are typical office hours in Australia?**
As in the UK, office hours vary from company to company, but it is common to start work at 8:30 in the morning and work through to 5 or 5:30 in the afternoon.

► **Will I get a cigarette break?**
Again, this depends on the company that employs you. However, Australia – like most other parts of the developed world – isn't very keen on smoking, so don't view cigarette breaks as any kind of entitlement.

► **What if I have a problem with working conditions?**
No job is ideal, and accepting this fact enables the vast majority of gappers to take the rough bits with the smooth. As a non-resident temporary or casual worker you should check out your legal rights as an employee on a site like *www.wagenet.gov.au*, or *www.workplace.gov.au* or speak to a recruitment consultant. However, if you have a serious problem with work (as opposed to a personal niggle) you should take steps to get it sorted. First, bring your problem to the attention of your employer as tactfully as you can. Communicating about problems is often the fastest way to sorting it out. If you are employed via a temp agency, approach your employer first and then speak with the agency if the problem isn't resolved. And, of course, if the problem is of a criminal nature (such as sexual harassment) you should report it to the police, just as you would here in the UK. An important thing to remember is to check that your travel insurance policy covers you for working. Many standard policies don't.

2 Travel Essentials

So, after finding out how you go about getting your work permit or visa, and what jobs you can do, you need to get some travel essentials sorted. It's very easy to get so wrapped up in the excitement of heading off to Oz that you end up forgetting some important things. Things like insurance might not seem the most glamorous subject to be thinking about, but if you break your leg in a freak water skiing accident and you've not got insurance, you could be paying for treatment for a very long time indeed. You also need to think about accommodation - sleeping on the beach, quite apart from probably being illegal, is not very much fun if you've been on a plane for the best part of 24 hours. *Australia Gap Pack* will help you get somewhere to stay. This section will also advise you about getting to and getting around Australia, plus help you with handy information on the best ways to keep everyone at home up-to-date and green with envy as you travel around. All this, plus advice with money and vital information on what to do if it all goes horribly wrong. Who better to help you do this than the experts?

Travel essentials at a glance

- Sort out the clothing and gear you will be taking.
- Cover yourself properly with an insurance policy.
- Book accommodation in advance to avoid the 'Mary and Joseph' syndrome.
- Find out about getting there.
- Find out about getting around once you've got there.
- Stay in touch with the aid of our communications pages.
- Keep track of your precious dollars in the money section.
- Make sure you know about travel safety issues (sounds boring but it's not – it could make the difference between a trip of a lifetime or a holiday from hell).
- And who to call if it all goes wrong in emergencies.

So read on, and enjoy! Got itchy feet yet? You obviously haven't read enough. And if you have any questions, why not email us: *info@gapwork.com*

Get your kit off

One of the most common questions asked by people thinking of going backpacking is – 'what do I need to take?' First of all, though, you need to think about what you're going to put it all in.

Buying a rucksack
Your first concern should be a rucksack. Two things are important when choosing your rucksack: the first is fit, and the second is capacity. The fit of the rucksack is vital because you are likely to be carrying it for a lot of the time. Wandering round a hot city, trying to find a hostel with a 60-litre pack straining at your shoulders is not a good way of starting your holiday. Only buy a rucksack after you have tried it on –

with weight in it. You are most likely to be buying a rucksack with an internally built frame, as these are good for comfort and balance. Frameless rucksacks are more likely to be used for daypacks or climbing and other activities where flexibility is required. Rucksacks with external frames are an older design and are most appropriate for very heavy loads that need to be piled high on the back.

When you are trying on your rucksack, all the weight should be on your hips rather than on your shoulders. You should feel the weight being carried around the small of your back. This is where your natural centre of balance is.

A problem with some internal framed rucksacks is that the surface against your back can prevent air circulation. This means that you'll have a hot, sweaty back – not what you need when trekking through a tropical rainforest! Make sure that any parts of the rucksack that will be in contact with your skin are made of breathable, open cell foam. This should assist air circulation. The size of the rucksack is equally important. Too big and you'll be tempted to pack your entire life into it before you go. Too small and you'll just end up buying a bigger rucksack later on in your travels. For a long journey expect to need a good 60-litre rucksack.

Most manufacturers have designed rucksacks especially for women. These are shorter in the back, slightly narrower and have different hip and belt adjustment straps. Another development is the Travel Pack, a kind of cross between a rucksack and a holdall. It looks like a rucksack, but has a zip down it and adjustable straps so you can carry it like a case if you need to. These tend to be more expensive, and bear in mind that the more zips you have on a rucksack, the more likely it is that water can get in – and zips can break. Travel packs can be a good option if you are not planning on doing a lot of real trekking or hiking, if you are planning on spending long periods in one place and if you need to arrive somewhere looking smarter than your average backpacker. When you have found a rucksack which is the right size, the right price and suitable for your journey, do a final check:

- Are the seams double or triple sewn?
- Are major seams covered or sealed?
- Is the rucksack as waterproof as possible?
- Is it made out of heavy-duty nylon?
- Is the base of the rucksack thicker than the rest of it?

What should I pack?

We've compiled an exhaustive travel checklist for you in our resources section at the back – we're not saying you have to take all of it, but it should be a useful guide to make sure you don't forget anything vital. Take a look at the tips that follow, and then don't forget to check out the checklist before you pack!

SOME BASIC TIPS
► Pack the heaviest stuff at the bottom and towards the inside of the rucksack (i.e. against your back).
► Pack the things which you will need most often near the top.
► Be ruthless. Books are heavy to carry and you can buy them anywhere; likewise toiletries.

If you are planning on going into the Outback or bush, the experts recommend that you pack the following:
- Water bottle (with water in it!).
- Survival knife (Swiss army multi-purpose type).
- Plastic bags for use as water collectors.
- Foil rescue blanket for shelter, warmth and as a signalling aid if you get into trouble.
- Nylon cord for multiple uses.
- Canvas tape for first aid and repairs.
- Hand mirror for signalling aid.

- Waterproof matches.
- Water purifying tablets.
- Barley sugar for energy food source.
- You should also bring a ground sheet and a sleeping bag liner if you are planning on camping. And a tent, obviously!

Female travellers

You've probably already developed your own personal strategies for dealing with aggressive, unpleasant men, and if they've worked for you in your home country, the chances are they'll work in Australia too. However, here are some additional guidelines:

- Walk confidently down the street and look as if you know where you're going (even if you don't!).
- Try and ignore comments and remarks, but don't ignore dangerous situations as they develop – never allow yourself to become isolated and vulnerable.
- Try not to be out and about on your own after dark, and be wary if you're drinking alone.
- Be careful of what you drink, how much you drink and make sure nobody puts anything in your drink.
- Stay close to other women if possible, whether in the street or on public transport.
- Never accept lifts or get into a car if you don't know the driver.

Gay and lesbian travellers

Australia, as you'd expect, is a pretty relaxed place, and this attitude makes it a great place for gay and lesbian travellers. As with most countries though, the further you get away from the large, cosmopolitan cities the less opened-minded some (and we stress 'some') people are. In general, though, Australia is one of the best destinations on the planet for gay and lesbian travellers, and plays host to unmissable events like the Sydney Gay and Lesbian Mardi Gras, one of the largest of its kind.

Insurance

Getting the proper insurance is vitally important for your trip. A good gap year policy will be tailored to the particular needs of backpackers. Your luggage as a backpacker is probably only going to consist of a rucksack with a few clothes, so most policies don't insure your luggage for a huge amount. The medical cover you receive is very important, as you may be travelling in developing countries, before reaching Australia, where the medical services are not up to western standards.

Even in developed countries, health services work differently and you may have to pay more for certain things. Medical treatment is very expensive wherever you are and if something really drastic happened to you while you were abroad, the costs could be astronomical. Most gap year insurance packages cover repatriation costs, meaning that they would pay for you to be flown home if you were seriously ill. Some

---

INSURANCE CHECKLIST

- How long am I insured for?
- Where in the world will the insurance policy cover me?
- What happens if I lose or have my passport stolen?
- What happens if someone steals my wallet?
- Am I covered for extreme sports, work and adventure activities?
- What happens if I need to go hospital?
- What happens if I miss my flight?
- What happens if I have to do exam retakes?
- Will I get flown home if I need to?

INSURANCE TIPS

▶ Take the contact phone number of your insurance company with you in case of emergency. Carry it around with you in your money belt, in your rucksack and in your wallet. Also copy the policy number and any other reference you will need if you have to contact them. Photocopy the insurance documents and take them with you on your travels. Read the small print on the policy – many policies don't cover you if you have an accident while on a motorbike and don't cover your property if it is left in a car overnight (unless it is locked in the boot).

▶ We also recommend checking out *www.travelvault.com* before you go. This site allows you to upload copies of all your important travel documents including passports, visas, travellers' cheques, etc. to a secure online storage area. You can then retrieve them via fax or email, when required, at any time from anywhere in the world.

will cover the cost of having a family member flown out to you in an emergency. Knowing you are covered for most eventualities gives you the peace of mind to really enjoy your gap year.

What the small print *really* says

It all seems so simple, but there are a few things you should always bear in mind before you hand over your cash for an insurance policy:

- If you've got an ongoing illness like asthma or diabetes, make sure your policy covers them (MOST DON'T).
- Ongoing medication and vaccinations are usually not covered.
- Dental treatment costs are usually for emergency treatment and agonizing pain relief only.
- If an insurance company says they'll fly you home in a medical emergency, bear in mind that it won't be up to you – the doctors and the insurance companies will decide how serious it is.

- If you can wait until you get home, it's unlikely your cover will cover any costs of treatment you think you might need.
- If you're going to do sports, make sure you're covered for that activity – don't just assume. Many companies make you pay extra for adventure sports insurance and hazardous activity insurance.
- If you're off your head when you hurt yourself then there's a good chance you'll foot the bill.
- If your airline goes bust you're unlikely to be covered – unless you've got Airline Failure Insurance. Make sure this is included when you buy your ticket.
- If you haven't got a receipt for a stolen item, you probably won't get anything back from the insurers.
- If you forget to report a theft to the police, you probably won't be covered for the loss.

MORE INSURANCE INFO

For more info, take a look at the Navigator Travel Insurance website: *www.navigatortravel.co.uk*

... and make sure you also check out these other great companies:
ACE TRAVEL INSURANCE *www.acetravelinsurance.com*
DOWN UNDER INSURANCE *www.duinsure.com*

Accommodation

Hostels
Hostels are by far the most popular type of accommodation for backpackers in Oz – and you can banish all thoughts of grim dormitories and curfews before you get there. The hostel industry in Australia is one of the most developed in the world, and you can expect hostels with bars, pools and even job centres!

► *www.hostelworld.com*
► *www.hostelaustralia.com*

Hostelworld.com offers instant online reservations at hundreds of hostels throughout Australia. And before booking, you can read details on all the hostels before you head off at *www.hostelworld.com*. *Hostelworld.com* also features hostel reviews from other travellers based on character, location, fun, security and staff. These are independent reviews from people who have already stayed in these hostels so they should give you a good indication of the standards.

There are no membership requirements to book online at *Hostelworld.com* but if you want to save money on your hostel bookings

TRAVEL ESSENTIALS

HOSTEL SAFETY

Following the tragedy at the hostel in Childers, Queensland in June 2000, awareness has been raised about hostel safety. Tourism New South Wales issue the following checklist to backpackers looking for hostel accommodation:

- Are there two escape routes from your room?
- Is there a working smoke alarm fitted in your room?
- Can you open the escape doors after hours (night time)?
- Does the window open for evacuation purposes?
- Is there an evacuation assembly area for the hostel?
- Are there loose light switches or electrical outlets?
- Is rubbish/trash piled up against the hostel?

Source: 'Safe Backpacking in New South Wales' leaflet. Go to: *www.visitnsw.com.au*

Ask yourself the following questions:

1. How much can I spend? Prices will vary according to the season, the individual hostel, and the type of room you want.

2. Where do I want to be? Do you want to stay in a city centre near bars and clubs? Or would you rather head for the quieter suburbs?

3. How long do I want to stay there? If you are planning on spending a long time in one place, you will need to look for short term rented accommodation payable by the month, not by the night.

4. Could I work there? If you are thinking of staying for a shorter time, but still long enough to see the bills mount up, you could negotiate a deal whereby you work in the hostel and get free accommodation.

5. What kind of room do I want? If you are travelling alone or in a group, a dormitory will definitely be the best option. If you are in a couple and need some privacy, you'll have to stump up more for a room.

6. What kind of hostel do I want? Some hostels are run by chains and have hundreds of beds run with lots of facilities – bar, off-licence, job centre, swimming pool etc. These tend to be in city centres and can be a bit impersonal if you are looking to make friends with fellow travellers or Australians. At the other end of the scale are small outfits that are often run by ex-travellers. In between comes everything else, but in the aftermath of the hostel fire in Queensland in 2000, safety is an issue. To be on the safe side, when you first arrive and need to get your bearings, prepare to pay a little more for a central hostel with a good reputation.

for a whole year, sign up now for Hostelworld's Gold Membership. Just $10 annually, it guarantees that you pay no $2 service charges on bookings over a 12-month period. Don't forget that Hostelworld.com also offers information and online bookings for all your tours and activities in Australia. So before you dive the reef, bus it up the East Coast or bungee-jump off a bridge, check out the best deals at *Hostelworld.com*.

Getting there

Flights
Buying your flight to Australia should be easy. Do so by calling into a high street travel agent or by using the Internet. Research prices online and in the adverts in the travel sections of newspapers before paying for a flight.

How much you pay depends on when you fly. The busiest times for flights are around school holidays in July, August and December, and this is when flights will be more expensive. The Australian spring begins in September and the summer ends in February, so this part of the year is also popular in terms of visitor arrivals. Travelling at Christmas can mean booking flights months in advance and paying more. If you were to wait until January, the price of flights will drop. Sydney is the most popular city to fly into.

Australia is a long way from the UK – a flight can take up to 25 hours, depending on your route. Stopovers in Bangkok or Singapore are the most popular option for backpackers.

Jet lag
One of the main problems with long-haul flights is that crossing time zones disrupts your sleep patterns and causes jet lag. Travelling eastwards is more likely to make you jetlagged than going west. Symptoms include tiredness, irritability, forgetfulness and disorientation. This can be a real problem if, as well as arriving in

a strange country, you have to cope with feeling jet lagged. You can help prevent jet lag by getting a good night's sleep the night before you travel, drinking plenty of water, stretching regularly during the flight and taking daytime flights. To give yourself time to adapt to new time zones and recover from jet lag, allow one day's recovery for every time zone you cross.

Economy class syndrome

Travelling for hours on a plane is not good for your circulation. Economy class syndrome is the commonly used name for deep vein thrombosis (DVT). DVT happens when a blood clot forms after being sat in cramped conditions for a long period of time. It is relatively rare, but research on the subject shows that it may be more of a problem than previously thought. The condition can be fatal. By simply moving around during the flight, walking up and down the aisle, stretching and drinking plenty of water, you reduce the chances of developing DVT. Taking sleeping pills or drinking excessive alcohol during the flight is not recommended. The more mobile and active you are, the better. Smokers, obese people and women who are pregnant or using the contraceptive pill are at more risk of developing DVT.

Getting around

Public transport

The alternative to organized tours designed for backpackers is taking public transport. The downside to public transport is that the routes are the quickest way of getting from A to B, rather than going to places of specific interest to travellers. And, of course, you don't have tour guides or pre-organized accommodation.

Greyhound buses

'The country's only national coach company', according to Greyhound Australia's website. Their Aussie Explorer passes are available at a discount with a recognized student/backpacker membership card (i.e. YHA, VIP or Nomads). With their Aussie Passes you can choose to either save money by buying up a bank of kilometres that you then use up as you travel or you can buy a pass that allows you to travel a set itinerary. The choice is yours.

CASE STUDY

TRAVELLING IN AUSTRALIA – KATE LEE

I came out to Australia purely to travel. I had decided not to get a working holiday visa due to the fact I would not be spending enough time in Australia to justify it. It's too risky to try and get a cash-in-hand job and the Aussies are pretty strict on who can work and who can't – there are so many tourists, they are able to pick and choose!

We travelled from Darwin down to Alice Springs and camped out, which was great fun – although I had a few worries about all the big spiders! Camping out under the stars near Ayers Rock was just brilliant! We then flew over to Sydney and took the Oz Experience bus from Sydney up to Cairns.

The bus is a great way to meet other like-minded people and see spots you probably wouldn't see if you were travelling by yourself. However, it can be a problem if you are limited for time, as there are so many other backpackers in Australia who also want a seat, so you need to plan ahead and book your space!

We spent six weeks in Australia and it was a bit of a hectic schedule. I would have liked to spend more time in Sydney – it's a fantastic city – and also the Whitsunday Islands; they are absolutely stunning!

We managed to fit in all sorts of activities (we also spent too much money) such as climbing the Harbour Bridge, taking a three-day sailing trip around the Whitsundays, visiting the Sydney Olympic Stadium, diving at the Great Barrier reef and walking around Ayers Rock watching the sun rise.

If I did it all again, I would take a camper van up the West coast, as I'm a bit older now and it's quieter than the excitement of the East coast! I would also get stuck in and try some voluntary conservation work.

Rail travel and flights are the other most popular ways of getting around Australia. The Indian Pacific train journey from Sydney to Perth and the Ghan route from Melbourne to Alice Springs are both world famous train journeys, taking in amazing scenery.

Recent developments in the internal flights market mean prices are very reasonable. However, it may be cheaper to book internal flights in advance with your travel agent before you arrive in Australia. See our Web Directory for listings of airlines and rail companies.

Tours

Australia is truly a backpacker paradise. As if it wasn't enough that it has beaches, desert and tropical rainforest all in one country, there are loads of great ways of getting to these places. Many backpackers and independent travellers choose to use the excellent backpacker bus networks that cross the country. These networks offer 'hop on, hop off' flexibility and more unusual destinations. The tours will also have a

TIPS

► Are you spending enough time in Australia to warrant getting a working holiday visa?

► Remember, Australia is a huge place. Give yourself enough time to travel round without rushing!

► When you plan your route, remember that most operators include a multi stop in Australia so if you are strapped for cash, you can often fit in an extra flight somewhere.

► If you don't have a working holiday visa, you can still try your hand at volunteering – it's great for the CV and you get to meet some new friends! Try *www.conservationvolunteers.com.au* or *www.wwoof.com.au*.

► When you work out your budget, remember Australia is an expensive place to visit and there's plenty to do, so your pound will not stretch very far.

driver and a guide who will help you on your travels. They are designed especially for independent travellers and the one thing they all have in common is that you will be travelling with lots of other like-minded people. Some tours are for the more committed off-the-beaten-track traveller, while others have a reputation for a wild party atmosphere. Check out the websites of the operators before you commit your cash, and make sure that you know what sort of tour you are buying a ticket for!

Driving

To drive in Australia you will need a full driving licence. You will need to carry your licence with you at all times – there is an on the spot fine for not doing so. Australians drive on the left hand side of the road, and the speed limits are 35mph/60kmph in built up areas and 60mph/100kmph on country roads and highways.

It is compulsory to wear seatbelts front and back at all times, and the laws on drink driving are enforced very strictly. Random breath testing is common, as are speed traps. Petrol costs between 90 and 120 cents per litre.

If you are planning on going off the beaten track then be sure that you have a full tank of fuel. Rural garages tend to shut earlier and may not take credit card payments. Driving is one of the best ways to see Australia and can be an unforgettable experience. Use your common sense when heading inland and into bush areas. Make sure you have plenty of supplies, including fuel, food and enough water for you and your car. Also leave your travel itinerary with a friend – make sure someone knows where you are planning on going and when you will get to your destination.

Many hire firms operate a one-way hire service, so you can hire from Cairns and drop off in Sydney. The minimum rental age is 21. One or two companies also offer a Buyback Guarantee on cars for sale, which means you are guaranteed a fixed amount when you sell your

REASONS TO DRIVE YOURSELF IN OZ

► If a group of two or three or more band together and share costs, then it is actually the cheapest form of travel possible.

► You can pull over and camp for free in many places.

► You don't have to pay extra for side trips, you can simply drive yourself.

► You can stop if you see something interesting.

► You can play your own tunes.

car back at the end of your trip. But beware of dodgy operators: try to ask other travellers about their experiences with particular firms. You can do this online by going to the Thorn Tree message boards at *www.lonelyplanet.com*.

If you are buying a vehicle when you arrive in Oz you will need to check the state registration requirements. There are official websites where you can check vehicle registration requirements, road laws and advice on driving in our Australia Backpacker Web Directory at the back of this book.

Hitching lifts is not recommended in any country. You are potentially leaving yourself open to all kinds of dangers, and who wants to be stuck in a lorry cab with a stranger for days in the middle of nowhere, anyway?

Driver fatigue is responsible for almost one fifth of fatal crashes in Australia. You should allow time for fifteen minute breaks every two hours on your journey. When you are driving long distances through countryside beware of the animals that often stray onto the road. Road kill is a common sight on the freeway, and we're talking six-foot kangaroos jumping out in front of your van...

Communications

Telecommunications

Phone kiosks are located in all public areas and hostels.

Peak call times are between 7am to 7pm Mon-Fri, standard rate calls are between 7pm to 7am and weekends.

Mobile phones

Buying a prepaid mobile phone in Australia will help you to be contactable for employers. If you are serious about working and staying in one place for any period of time, try and budget for a phone. Another alternative is to get a foreign SIM card, which allows you to use your own phone abroad for cheaper calls while you're in Australia. By using a 0044 foreign SIM card in your mobile phone you can avoid all

USEFUL NUMBERS

- To call Oz from abroad dial 0061 + area code (drop the zero) + number.
- Area Codes: Brisbane 07, Melbourne 03, Perth 08, Sydney 02, Byron Bay 02, Geelong 03, Cairns 07, Gold Coast 07, Bunbury 08, Adelaide 08, Barossa Valley 08, Darwin 08, Alice Springs 08, Canberra 02, Hobart 03
- To call the UK from Oz dial 0044 + area code (without the first 0) + number.
- To call Ireland from Oz dial 00353 + area code (without the first 0) + number.
- To call Canada from Oz dial 001 + the 10 digit number.
- International Operator 1225.
- Operator 013 for a number in an area you are currently in.
- 0175 for a number somewhere else in Australia.
- Emergency Services 000.

MOBILE SIM CARD INFO

www.0044.co.uk
www.sim4travel.com

....

You could also check out your mobile phone operator's website to find out more about roaming options on your phone:

3 – *www.three.co.uk*

VODAFONE – *www.vodafone.co.uk*

ORANGE – *www.orange.co.uk*

O2 – *www.o2.co.uk*

T-MOBILE – *www.t-mobile.co.uk*

roaming charges, make outgoing calls at local rates and receive calls for free. SIM4travel also offer similar deals on their SIM cards.

If you take your own mobile, make sure it is dual band at least. Dual band allows your phone to work in over 150 countries, but if you are thinking about travelling to the Americas, you'll need a quad-band phone to both South and North America due to newly allocated frequencies that are used over there.

Landlines

Buy a phonecard and call home from a payphone. Check out some of these sites for more info: *www.card4anywhere.com; www.iscard.com*

Skype

A great way to call home without paying a fortune is to use Skype. This is a free computer application which allows any two people with a PC and an internet connection to make a 'virtual phone call' over cyberspace. The negligible cost of calls made in this way beat long-distance charges hands down, so if think you will have computer and internet access in Australia, check out *www.skype.com*.

Online

Probably the easiest and most convenient way to keep in contact with those you've left behind. You can find internet cafes all over the world and their rates are mostly very cheap. So get typing! Try the numerous online photo albums and travel blogs that are out there.

Web-based email
FASTMAIL – *www.fastmail.co.uk*
YAHOO – *www.yahoo.co.uk*
MSN HOTMAIL – *www.msn.com*
CARE2 EMAIL – *www.care2.com*

Blogging and online photo journals
MyTripJournal.com: MyTripJournal.com gives you the space to build your own travel website while you're on your gap year. You can write about your experiences, map out your trip and upload photos for your family and friends to drool over! Make sure you sign up before you go. *www.mytripjournal.com*

You could also try these sites:
TRAVEL BLOG – *www.travelblog.org*
TRAVEL POST – *www.travelpost.com*
MY WORLD JOURNAL – *www.myworldjournal.com*
BLOGGER – *www.blogger.com*

Money

Exchange rates

The Australian Dollar is divided into 100 cents, and one British pound will normally buy more than two Aussie dollars. For the very latest exchange rates, check out *www.oanda.com*. And while we're on the subject, be careful to shop around when exchanging your pounds for dollars. Banks and bureaux de change will charge different fees for

TRAVEL ESSENTIALS

Banana bender – person from Queensland (we have no idea!)
Bastard – a term of endearment apparently
Battler – someone who works hard on low pay
Bitzer – a mongrel dog (bits of this, bits of that)
Bloody oath – certainly!
Bludger – blagger
Bonzer – great!
Brizzie – short for Brisbane
Click – kilometre
Crook – poorly
Dill – prat
Dipstick – origin of 'dippy'
Drongo – idiot
Durry – cigarette
Drum – info, as in grapevine
Feral – someone a bit alternative
Galah – fool. Named after the bird which flies south in winter (when its hot in Oz)
Going off – banging, as in 'the party was banging'
Grog – booze
Hoon – hooligan
Kangaroo loose in top paddock – few sandwiches short of a full picnic

Liquid laugh – puke
The lucky country – Australia, presumably for having so many Brits visiting
Moolah – cash
Ocker – pleb
Pommy – Brit
Pommy shower – using deodorant without bothering to shower
Rage – having it large
Rapt – pleased as punch
Sandgroper – someone from Western Australia
Shark biscuit – novice surfer
Shonky – dodgy
Slab – 24 cans of lager
Snag – sausage
Spunk – totty
Station – a big farm
Strides – trousers
Tall poppies – successful people
Thongs – flip flops
Top end – northernmost bit of Oz
Tucker – food
Ute – Utility vehicle
Wowser – boring person
Yakka – work

Thanks to *www.koalanet.com.au* for their contributions – cheers mateys!

changing your cash. Some ways of changing money (such as credit cards) might seem convenient, but they can also be costly and incur a surcharge or give you a poor exchange rate for the privilege of using them!

If you intend carrying a lot of cash on your person (this could be the case if you don't want to open an Aussie bank account), consider getting traveller's cheques as a safer alternative. Traveller's cheques also make it easier to keep track of what you are spending and budgeting.

Check with your bank at home to find out if you can withdraw money from cash machines (ATMs) in Australia using your credit or debit card and, if so, what the charges will be. Some debit cards such as Cirrus and Visa debit work in countries across the world. It is also worth asking your home bank if they have any links with Australian banks, which mean that you can withdraw money from cash machines in Australia with no charges.

Bank accounts

Opening a bank account in Australia is necessary if you want to work for agencies or established businesses. You will need a passport and a permanent address. The banks listed in this book under the relevant destinations are the larger ones which have the most branches nationwide. The branch listed is just one of the more centrally located in each city.

The points system

Australian Banks require you to fulfil a 'points' score for ID purposes before you open an account with them. There is nothing sinister about this. Basically you need 100 points to open an account. Your passport is worth 60 points. A driving licence with photo is worth 40 points. So if you have these then you're sorted! If you don't have a driving licence, then a birth certificate is also worth 40 points, a Switch card or Visa card is worth 25. However you do it, opening a bank account in Australia is actually easier than opening one in the UK. Do try to get a bank account sorted out in the first few weeks of arriving in Australia. The longer you leave it, the more difficult it is to arrange.

EFTPOS is an Australian kind of debit card – particularly useful for supermarket shopping and using in cash points. You may be offered one with your Aussie bank account.

Getting a permanent address

You will need a permanent address to get a bank account and tax file number. Permanent addresses are defined differently depending on the bank, but most travellers use either a PO Box, a holding address, a hostel address or the address of a friend in Australia.

Healthcare and emergencies

Hospitals and medical centres
For emergencies dial 000. If you need medical advice for minor problems, chemists are a good source of information. Each destination in this book has hospitals listed in the 'Support' section.

Medicare
Medicare is the Oz version of the NHS. You will need to enrol at a Medicare office to get your card, and then you can get free hospital

MEDICARE OFFICES
Sydney Shop 30 Town Hall Arcade, 464–480 Kent Street
Brisbane Shop 47-48, Wintergarden Queen Street,
Brisbane QLD 4000
Melbourne Ground Floor, 460 Bourke Street
Perth Wesley Centre, First Floor, Wesley Arcade, 93 William Street

treatment for emergencies and a refund on some doctors' charges. It is still important to take out adequate health insurance before you leave the UK. You can call the Medicare Information Service on 13 2011 in Australia.

Health tips

Sunbathing may be high on your list of things to do while in Australia, but be aware of the risks inherent in catching those southern hemisphere rays. Australia sits below a massive hole in the ozone layer and consequently it has the highest skin cancer rate in the world. It's been known for your skin to begin to burn as soon as you become exposed (we're talking seconds not hours here). You'll notice that a lot of the natives wear long, light clothing, hats and, of course, lots of sun cream because of that. Even people with a darker complexion should use a sun cream with a high SPF (25 or more) throughout the day, and between 11am and 3pm the shade is the safest place to be. Hats are always a good option, and to prevent dehydration drink plenty of water.

Sex

If you intend getting jiggy in Australia, practise safe sex. All forms of contraception are available in Australia from most General Practitioners and Family Planning Clinics. To locate the closest Family Planning Clinic to you, contact:
FPA Health
328-336 Liverpool Road
Ashfield NSW
Phone: +61 (0)2 9716 6099
or +61 (0)2 9916 8313
or 1300 658 886 (within Australia)

The most convenient forms of contraception are most probably going to be the contraceptive pill and condoms, as these can be stocked up on before you go.

Unfortunately, Australia is like almost every other country in the world: sexually transmitted diseases (STDs) are becoming more commonplace in the 15-35 age bracket. The vast majority of STDs can be easily treated by a doctor, Sexual Health Clinic (which are attached to the public hospitals) or a Family Planning Clinic. And please don't feel embarrassed about visiting a clinic for an STD: they deal with these problems all the time and will respect you more for being sensible and seeking advice.

Embassies

Your embassy can help you out in a number of ways if you get into trouble or fall seriously ill while you're abroad. They can contact your relatives, issue emergency passports and help you transfer money. If you need a doctor or a lawyer, they can find one for you. They can even loan you enough money to get home in desperate circumstances. Hopefully you won't have to call on them!

To reduce the chances of having an accident, falling ill or being the victim of crime when abroad, check the British Foreign and Commonwealth Office website at: *www.fco.gov.uk/knowbeforeyougo*.

The 'Know Before You Go' campaign was set up by the Foreign Office in order to reduce the number of travellers going to their overseas consuls with problems that could have been prevented. The aim of the campaign is to raise traveller's awareness of the issues that need to be sorted out before they leave the country.

British High Commission
Commonwealth Avenue, Yarralumla, ACT 2600
Tel: (02) 6270 6666

British Consulate in Sydney
Level 16, The Gateway, Level UK (16), 1 Macquarie Place, Sydney, NSW 2000. Tel: (02) 9247 7521
Contact online at *http://bhc.britaus.net/*

British Consulate in Brisbane
Level 26, Waterfront Place, 1 Eagle Street, Brisbane QLD 4000
Tel: (07) 3223 3200
Contact online at *http://bhc.britaus.net/*

British Consulate in Melbourne
17th Floor 90 Collins Street, Melbourne, Victoria 3000
Tel: (03) 9652 1670
bcgmelb@hotkey.net.au

(For Hobart, contact the Consulate in Melbourne)

British Consulate in Adelaide
Level 22, Grenfell Centre, 25 Grenfell St, Adelaide 5000
Tel: (08) 8212 7280

British Consulate General
Level 26, Allendale Square, 77 St Georges Terrace, Perth WA 6000
Tel: (08) 9224 4770

Canadian Consulate General
Level 5, 111 Harrington Street, Sydney
Tel: (02) 9364 3000
sydny@dfait-maeci.gc.ca

Canadian Consulate
3rd Floor, 267 St Georges Terrace, Perth WA
Tel: (08) 9322 7930

Consulate of Canada
123 Camberwell Road, Hawthorn, East Victoria
Tel: (03) 9811 9999

Irish Consulate General
Level 30, 400 George Street, Sydney, NSW 2000
Tel: (02) 9231 6999
consyd@ireland.com

Irish Consulate
10 Lilika Road, Perth, WA
Tel: (08) 9385 8247

Travel safety

Looking after your belongings
There are few things worse than losing your rucksack or belongings when you are away. There will be times when you have to leave your rucksack in vulnerable places, and you'll feel much happier about doing this if you have some security items to try and keep it as safe and protected as possible. Below are some products we recommend:

- **Rucksack harness** – protects your rucksack from damage and theft both in transit and when being worn. It is expensive, but think about how much it would cost to replace your rucksack, and everything it contains, if it was lost or stolen.
- **Waist wallet** – for documents and money. Ideally it should be worn against the skin for total concealment. Try not to have to access a waist wallet when you are in a public place, especially in a bus or train station.
- **Cable lock** – for securing luggage or skis to an immoveable object.
- **Padlocks** – ideally with combination rather than key.
- **Personal attack alarm**
- **Door guard** – simple gadget that secures an inward opening door.
- **Waterproof wallets and cases** – there are many types available, not only for money and documents but also for mobile phones.
- **First aid kit** – whether you are stuck in a city centre hostel or out in the mountains hiking, this will be useful.

Creepy crawlies

Australia is home to lots of weird, scary and dangerous stuff. Don't let this put you off – incidents of being bitten by a spider or snake are rare. But if you really want to know what's lurking underfoot, then read on.

Redback spider

Australia's most common venomous spider, this little nipper leads to 200 people every year requiring treatment for bites. Symptoms include sweating, paralysis, stiffness and tremors. The spider has a distinctive, hour-glass shaped mark under its abdomen, and a red or orange stripe on the upper abdomen.

The Common Huntsman spider

There are two kinds of Huntsman spider: the Common variety and the Shield. Both live under loose bark, but given half the chance will settle into a house. They are grey to brown in colour with a flattened body. The bite isn't dangerous but the Shield Huntsman's bite can be painful. We don't like this one because it can grow up to 15cm in leg span.

The Funnel Web

The world's most deadly spider. They live in Eastern Australia and Tasmania and like hiding under logs, in tree holes and in your back garden. The body length can go up to 4.5cm and they are dark coloured.

SCARY FACTS

► 9 of the 10 most venomous snakes in the world live in Australia.
► Box jellyfish swim in the seas around tropical Northern Australia at certain times of the year. Their sting can cause cardiac arrest.
► What with spiders, snakes and jellyfish, sharks are the least of your worries. (You are statistically more likely to be bitten by another human than by a shark!)
More info: *www.qmuseum.qld.gov.au*, *www.austmus.gov.au*

A Funnel Web's bites can cause serious illness and death. The symptoms begin with local pain, mouth numbness, vomiting, sweating and stomach pain. The good news is that anti-venom is available and since its introduction, no one has died from a Funnel Web bite.

Poisons Information Service:
The number is 13 11 26 in every state.

Staying safe in the Outback

The Outback is a pretty wild place – in fact, it's one of the wildest, hottest, driest and potentially most deadly environments on the planet. That said, it's also staggeringly beautiful, and should not be missed if you're heading Down Under. We've donned our sun hats, put on our desert boots and gathered together our essential tips for surviving the Outback.

- Make sure you have a good map with water sources marked on it, a compass, a GPS and an emergency position indicator radio beacon (EPIRB).
- Don't forget to tell people where you're going and when you're due back.
- Make sure you know your vehicle inside out and that you have all the spares you might need.
- If you do break down, don't panic. Stay calm and near your vehicle.
- Beware of animals on the tracks – hitting a cow or sheep at high speed will kill the animal, wreck your vehicle and leave you stranded, injured or even dead.
- Be ultra careful when you're crossing water – wade through it to check out how deep it is, but also be very aware that there may be crocodiles in the area.

Staying safe in the sea

With talk of deadly spiders, crocodiles and snakes, you'd think you might be safest in the water. And you're probably right – but the seas around Australia do hold certain dangers that you should be aware of.

Strong tides

These are potential killers. If you find yourself caught in a 'rip' as they are called, don't panic but try and float to the surface, putting your arm up to attract attention. Always pay attention to the flags on the beaches, as these will tell you where it is safe to swim and where there are life guards who will help you if you get into trouble.

Box jellyfish

A funny name for what is a very serious poisonous creature. Potentially deadly, they are up to 3m long and have a frightening number of stinging tentacles. They are quite hard to spot, so be very aware of their potential danger. In Northern Australia, box jellyfish season runs from October to April. Further south into Northern Queensland or northern Western Australia the season runs from November to March. Always check with local authorities about box jellyfish activity when you are in these parts of the country and fancy a dip in the sea.

Sharks

A no-brainer really – if you see a shark, stay away from it and tell someone. Shark attacks are not as common as the media would like to think, but it's worth bearing in mind that these beautiful but scary creatures do live in the waters around Australia. Talk to people, find out where they might be and try and see them from the safety of an organised shark viewing tour.

And finally...

Please don't be put off! You could argue that there are lots of ways for you to kill or injure yourself in Australia, from sunstroke to being bitten by deadly spiders. All of them are extremely unlikely to happen to you and any fear of them should just encourage you to be prepared and informed. Don't let knowing about potential dangers put you off getting out there and enjoying yourself!!!

For more info: *www.fco.gov.uk/travel*

3 Town by Town

New South Wales

From the desolate but beautiful Outback to the skiing in the Snowy Mountains, the variety of things you can get up to in New South Wales is incredible. As well as loads of opportunities for outdoor activities, there's plenty to do in Sydney itself. In fact, many people spend much of their time in New South Wales in one of the most exciting cities in the world. Whether you fancy rock climbing in the Blue Mountains, living and working in cosmopolitan Sydney or just heading into the Outback for an adventure, then New South Wales has it all.

Sydney

Why Sydney?

Ask most people what the capital of Australia is and you'll be surprised at how many people say Sydney (although they're wrong – it's Canberra). Arguably Australia's most famous city, Sydney is home to some of Australia's most famous sights. It is not just about surfing and sun-worshipping (although you've come to the right place if that's what you fancy!). You can't miss the Harbour Bridge or the Opera House, but there's plenty more to keep you entertained. Quite apart

---

SOME SYDNEY FACTS

► The city was named after a chap called Thomas Townsend. Work that one out...

► Sydney's Opera House was designed by a Dane called Jorn Utzon.

75

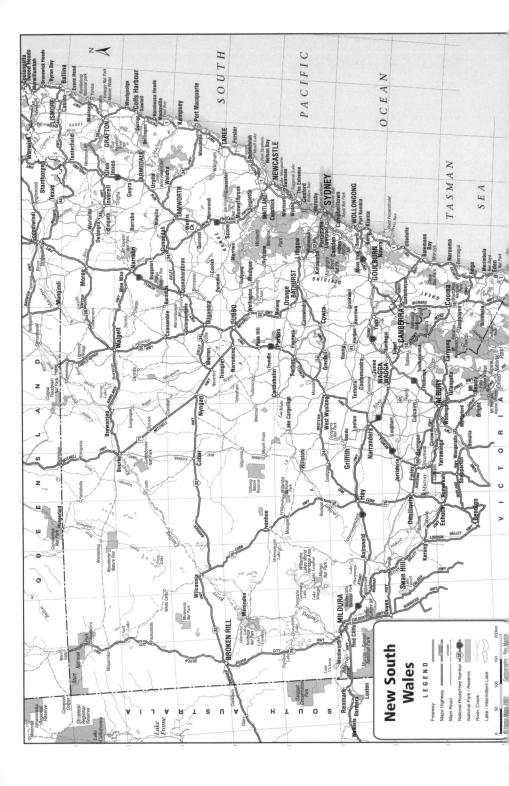

New South Wales

LEGEND

Freeway
Major Highway
Main Road
National Route/Hwy Number
National Park / Reserve
River, Creek
Lake / Intermittent Lake

0 50 100 150 200km

© Hema Maps 2001   Cartography : Rev Martin

from being home to some world-class museums (don't miss the Aboriginal works in the Art Gallery of NSW and the Australian Museum), it's also well worth seeing an opera at the Opera House. That said, it's also got some great bars, some of the finest places to eat out in Australia and fantastic weather. It's hard to beat.

Getting to and around Sydney

Bus: Many shuttle bus companies provide transport between the airport and most Sydney suburbs and regional areas. These buses need to be pre-booked. Check the Yellow Pages under 'Bus and Coach Services' for the service to and from your area. Sydney Buses has a timetables service between Bondi Junction and Burwood, which includes the T1 International and T3 Domestic Terminals in the route. Bus stops are located on the arrivals level of each of these terminals. Information about fares, timetables and connections to other parts of Sydney is available at *www.sydneybuses.info.*

Taxi: Each terminal has its own taxi rank with supervisors in case you have any problems. From the airport, you should expect to pay Sydney City $25, North Sydney $35, Manly $50.

Train: There are rail stations located at both the International and Domestic Terminals. Trains run approximately every 10 minutes and the journey into the city takes only 13 minutes. The international and domestic rail stations link directly to the City Circle, which means most city destinations are within a short walk of stations. Tickets can be purchased to all Sydney stations from the International and Domestic rail stations. Passengers can also transfer between terminals for a cost of $4.

Accommodation

Rentals
McGrath
Eastern Suburbs (Head Office)
191 New South Head Road, Edgecliff, NSW 2027
Tel: (02) 9386 3333
Fax: (02) 9386 3344
Website: *www.mcgrath.com.au*

First National
Level 1, 283 George Street, Sydney, NSW 2000
Tel: (02) 9262 3300
Fax: (02) 9262 3313
Email: nsw@firstnational.com.au
Website: *http://www.firstnational.com.au/*

Hostels
Bondi Beach
Biltmore on Bondi 110 Campbell Parade, Bondi Beach –1800 684 660
Bondi Lodge 63 Fletcher Street – (02) 9365 2088
Sinclair's of Bondi 11 Bennett Street – (02) 9744 6074

City
Central YHA Pitt Street, Sydney – (02) 9281 9111
Nomads City Central Backpackers 752 George Street – (02) 9212 4833
Wake Up 509 Pitt Street – (02) 9262 9705
Wanderers on Kent 477 Kent Street – (02) 9267 7718

Coogee
Aegean Coogee Bay Road Backpackers, 40 Coogee Bay Road –
　　(02) 9314 5324
Coogee Beach Backpackers 94 Beach Street, Coogee – (02) 9315 8000

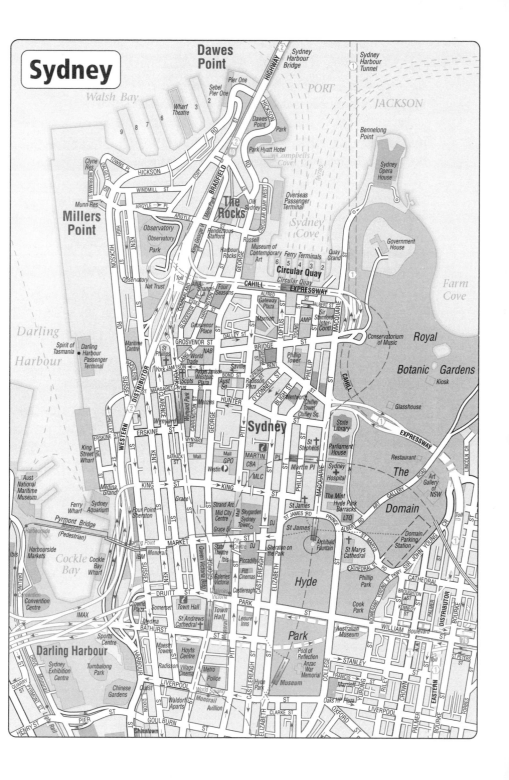

Indy's at Coogee Beach 302 Arden Street, Coogee – (02) 9315 7644
Surfside Backpackers 186 Arden Street, Coogee – (02) 9315 7888
Wizard of Oz 172 Coogee Bay Road, Coogee – (02) 9315 7876

Kings Cross
Boomerang Backpackers 141 William Street Kings Cross –
    (02) 8334 0488
Funk House Hostel 23 Darlinghurst Road Kings Cross – (02) 9358 6455
Hancock Hostel 48a Darlinghurst Road Kings Cross – (02) 9357 2255
Original Kings Cross Backpackers 162 Victoria Street – (02) 9356 3232
The Globe 40 Darlinghurst Road – (02) 9326 9675
The Palms 23 Hughes Street – FREECALL IN OZ – 1800 737 773
    or (02) 9357 1199 (International)

TIP
▶ If you have a credit card, you can book your first few nights in some
hostels over the phone or internet. Go to: *www.hostelsydney.com*

Work

Harvest work in New South Wales
Below are a few places where it's possible to get a job fruit picking in
New South Wales, along with all the best times to go and how far
away they are from the major cities. For a more expansive list, visit
www.jobsearch.gov.au/harvesttrail/ where jobs are listed and frequently
updated, plus you're getting information galore on each town.

Tumbarumba
Tumbarumba is situated 511km south-west of Sydney and 462km
north-east of Melbourne, among the western foothills of the Snowy
Mountains and a short distance from the Hume Highway.

January to March - *stone fruit*
March to May - *apples and grapes*
April and May - *chestnuts*
December - *cherries*
December to April - *berries*

Leeton
Leeton is located 595km west of Sydney.
January to December - *grapes*
January to December - *citrus fruits*

Office work
ASSIST - (02) 9413 2277
BOSS - (02) 9221 4399
DRAKE OVERLOAD - (02) 9273 0500
HALLIS - (02) 9241 3966
HAYS - (02) 9957 5763
INTEGRATED - (02) 9299 5477
IPA - (02) 9220 6900
JULIA ROSS - (02) 8256 0000
OPTIONS CONSULTING - (02) 9221 7733
PACE PERSONNEL - (02) 9299 9909
PIVOTAL - (02) 9267 9292
REDDIN - (02) 9233 7755
STRICTLY PERSONNEL - (02) 9413 2842

Accountancy
ACCOUNTANTS TASKFORCE - (02) 9223 5222
FSS FINANCIAL - (02) 9238 2133
LINK - (02) 9279 1511
MANPOWER - 132 502
PARKER BRIDGE - (02) 9299 9330
RECRUITMENT SOLUTIONS - (02) 8235 9666
ROBERT WALTERS - (02) 9231 3302

► 'Make sure you come to us with all the basics; an up-to-date resumé, references with contactable referees, a valid working holiday visa and a passport. Ideally you should have at least one year's experience in an office environment and have basic computer skills, including Microsoft applications. You'll be tested on your skills at interview – so be prepared!'

Yvonne Wilson, Senior Account Manager,
Strictly Personnel, Sydney

IT

HAYS IT – (02) 9235 1844
PRINCEPS – (02) 9956 5222
PROGRESSIVE PEOPLE – (02) 9957 1477
TALENT INTERNATIONAL – (02) 92414545

Hospitality employers

Bars that may employ travellers with Working Holiday Makers (WHM) visas

Arizona Bar 237 Pitt Street – (02) 9261 1077
East Village 243 Palmer Street East Sydney – (02) 9331 5457
Forresters Bar 336 Riley Street Surry Hills – (02) 9211 2095
Home Nightclub 101 Cockle Bay Harbour – (02) 9266 0600
La Campana 53 Liverpool Street – (02) 9267 3787
Lord Nelson 19 Kent Street – (02) 9251 4044
Mint Room 53 Martin Place – (02) 9233 5388
PJ Gallagher's 74 Church Street Parramatta – (02) 9635 8811
Planet Hollywood 600 George Street – (02) 9267 7827
Watson Bay Hotel 2 Military Road – (02) 9337 4299

Sydney hotels that may employ travellers on WHM visas

Civic Hotel 388 Pitt Street – (02) 8267 3183

TOWN BY TOWN

Dolphin On Crown Hotel 412 Crown Street Surry Hills – (02) 9331 4800
Mclaren Hotel North Sydney – (02) 995 44622
North Shore Hotel North Sydney – (02) 99551012

Agencies

ALSEASONS HOSPITALITY – (02) 9324 4666
SKILLED PERSONNEL – 1300 366 606
LLEM PERSONNEL – (02) 9233 3226
TROYS HOSPITALITY STAFF – (02) 9290 2955

CASE STUDY

MATT JORDAN, 26

I came out to Australia in August 2003 with two friends. Two of us had working holiday visas, the third was an Australian citizen who I had been at uni with in England. We arrived in Manly in early September and due to it being the end of the Australian winter, accommodation was easy to find. It also helped that we were prepared to take a six-month lease.

My English housemate instantly got a job in a local cafe and shortly after, my Australian friend got a full time permanent position in a big clothes store. I spent September and October handing out CVs in my local area and in the huge Mall nearby, looking for shop work. I'm 26 years old and my CV is not too shabby. I have experience in retail and pub work. I have a degree and I came out to Australia with some good references. I had maybe two interviews, both of which came to nothing due to my visa restrictions.

I then started to look for bar work, which was my back up plan, and it was much easier. I applied to three large hotels (Australian pubs) in Manly and got a trial at one. I proved myself there, and then started to get shifts. They work you very hard (long shifts in excess of 12 hours on weekends) and have very little work in the week. So on average I do maybe 25 hours a week.

As far as wages go, in shops they all pay around $14 an hour; in my bar I get $16 on weekdays, $19 on Saturdays and $22 on Sundays.

TOWN BY TOWN

Nursing
Agencies
CAMPAIGN NURSING – (02) 9241 3675
DIAL A NURSE – (02) 9572 9311
DRAKE MEDOX – (02) 9273 0501
GORDON NURSES – (02) 9953 9388
ID MEDICAL STAFFING – (02) 9957 1166
MEDICAL RECRUITMENT – (02) 9232 0700
MEDISTAFF – 1800 676 856
NURSING EXCELLENCE – (02) 9552 3975

You will need to register as a nurse at:
New South Wales State Nursing Registration Board, PO Box K599, Haymarket NSW 2001
Tel: (02) 9219 0222
nursesreg@doh.health.nsw.gov.au

For more information contact:
State Government Overseas Qualifications Unit
Qualifications Officer, Ground Floor, 255 Elizabeth Street, Sydney NSW 2000
Tel: (02) 9269 3500

TIP
► Some agencies recruit all kinds of medical staff, including administrative people.

Teaching
Agencies
DRAKE OVERLOAD – (02) 9273 0500
SELECT EDUCATION – (02) 8258 9800
TIMEPLAN – (02) 9838 0148

Independent schools

Association of Independent Schools New South Wales

Tel: (02) 9299 2845

Contact individual employers for vacancies in independent schools in New South Wales.

For information on registering as a teacher in New South Wales:
www.schools.nsw.edu.au – New South Wales Education Authority

TOP TIPS

► Bring references for work and personal ones for finding accommodation if you have them.

► You'll get a trial before you start a job. Work HARD!

► Befriend Australians – many jobs are found purely by word of mouth.

► When handing out your CV ask to give it to the manager. Many end up in the bin at the end of a shift!

► It's a different country, so don't expect it to be exactly like working in the UK.

► If all else fails you will get work fruit picking, in a factory or in a bar.

Support

Backpackers Travel Centre
Shop P33, Pitt Street Mall
Tel: (02) 9231 3699

Travellers Contact Point
Level 7 Dymocks Building, 428 George Street
Tel: (02) 9221 8744

Internet cafes
Backpackers World 212 Victoria Street – (02) 9380 2700
Global Gossip 111 Darlinghurst Road/14 Wentworth Ave/770 George Street – (02) 9326 9777
Internet Backpack Travel 3 Orwell Street – (02) 9360 3888
Student Uni Travel Level 8, 92 Pitt Street – (02) 9232 8444
Well Connected 35 Glebe Point, Glebe – (02) 9566 2655
Internet Café Hotel Sweeney's, 236 Clarence Street – (02) 9261 5666

Banks
ANZ – 275 George Street – 131314
Commonwealth – 254 George Street, Sydney, NSW 2000
Westpac – 341 George Street, Sydney, NSW 2000

Hospitals
Sydney Hospital, Macquarie Street – (02) 9382 7111
Travellers Medical & Vaccination Centre – (02) 9221 7133

If you are a victim of crime or need community advice:
NSW Police Service
Headquarters – 14-24 College Street, Darlinghurst, NSW 2010
Tel: (02) 9339 0277
Tel: 131444 for non-emergency
Tel: 000 Emergency

TOP TRAVEL SAFETY TIP
► Don't hang your backpack on the back of your chair in restaurants or bars. Keep any bags under your chair and loop a strap around a chair or table leg. This will prevent it being snatched.

► During the first half of the week, many youth orientated bars and pubs in Australian cities have 'backpacker nights', meaning drinks are cheap, music is cheesy and barbecues are free.
► To call Sydney from the UK and Ireland dial 0061+2+eight digit no.

Cool places to hang out...
Cafe Amsterdam 9A Roslyn Street, Kings Cross – (02) 8356 9018
Coogee Bay Hotel Coogee Bay Road – (02) 9665 0000
Home 101 Cockle Bay Wharf, Darling Harbour – (02) 9266 0600
Ice Box 2 Kellet Street, Kings Cross – (02) 9331 0058
Jackson's on George 176 George Street City – (02) 9247 2727
Lord Nelson Corner of Kent and Argyle Street, The Rocks –
    (02) 9251 4044
Rattlesnake Grill 130 Military Road, Neutral Bay – (02) 9953 4789
Scubar Corner of Rawson Lane and Rawson Place – (02) 9212 4244
Watson Bay Hotel 2 Military Road – (02) 9337 4299

Things to do in Sydney...
• Climb the Harbour Bridge.
• Look at the Opera House.
• Visit the Blue Mountains.
• Take a Harbour Cruise.
• Go to Fox Studios.
• Visit Taronga Zoo.
• Go to Sydney Aquarium.
• Check out Bondi Beach.
• Take a stroll through the Botanic Gardens.

To avoid spending loads of money...
• Walk across the bridge for free.
• Don't go in the opera house.

- Take a ferry round the harbour, not a cruise.
- Eat in cheaper suburbs like Newtown.
- Don't be afraid to look for less expensive accommodation outside the city.

Visitor Information Centre:
106 George Street, The Rocks – (02) 9255 1788

. . . .

Byron Bay

Why Byron Bay?
Byron Bay is about an hour and a half from the Gold Coast and is stunningly beautiful with a balmy sub-tropical climate. It has great beaches and great surfing, as well as opportunities to go bush walking and hiking.

Accommodation

Rentals
First National Real Estate
15 Lawson Street, Byron Bay NSW 2481
Tel: (02) 6685 8466 (24 hrs)
Email: *rental@byronbayfn.com*
Website: *www.byronbayfn.com*

SOME BYRON BAY FACTS
► It is Australia's most easterly point
► Paul Hogan (aka Crocodile Dundee) is from Byron Bay

Ed Silk Real Estate
8 Lawson Street, PO Box 627, Byron Bay NSW
Tel: (02) 6685 7000
Website: *www.edsilk.com.au*

Hostels
Aquarius Backpackers Resort 16 Lawson Street – (02) 6685 7663 or
1800 028 909 *www.aquarius-backpack.com.au, aquarius@om.com.au*
Arts Factory Backpackers Skinners Shoot Road – (02) 6685 7709
www.artsfactory.com.au, info@artsfactory.com.au
Backpackers Inn on the Beach 29 Shirley Street – (02) 6685 8231
www.byron-bay.com/backpackersinn
Belongil Beachhouse Childe Street – (02) 6685 7868
Byron Bay Bunkhouse 1 Carlyle Street – (02) 6685 8311
www.byronbay-bunkhouse.com.au, byronbay@nrg.com.au
Cape Byron Lodge 78 Bangalow Road – (02) 6685 6445
Holiday Village Backpackers 116 Jonson Street – (02) 6685 8888
J's Bay Hostel YHA 7 Carlyle Street – (02) 6685 8853 or 1800 678 195
Nomads Main Beach Backpackers Corner of Fletcher Street and Lawson
Street – (02) 6685 8695 or 1800 150 233

TIP
▶ If you have a credit card, you can book your first few nights in
some hostels in Byron Bay over the phone or internet. Go to:
www.hostelsydney.com

Work

Office work
WORKDIRECTIONS AUSTRALIA – (02) 6639 7777
ON-Q HUMAN – (02) 6685 5733

Hospitality employers
Bars that may employ travellers with Working Holiday Makers (WHM) visas
Beach Hotel – (02) 6685 64(02)
Byron Bay Bowling Club – (02) 6685 62(02)
Byron Bay Golf Club – (02) 6685 6470
Byron Bay Services Club – (02) 6685 6878
Great Northern Fine Wine & Liquor – (02) 6685 6454
Railway Friendly Bar – (02) 6685 7662; (02) 6685 7683
The Carpark – (02) 6685 6170

Byron Bay hotels that may employ travellers on WHM visas
Great Northern Hotel – (02) 6685 6454
Hibiscus Motel – (02) 6685 6195
Lord Byron Resort – (02) 6685 7444
Motel Cape Byron Resort – (02) 6685 7663
Newall's Apartments – (02) 6687 5144
Peppers Casuarina Lodge – 1800 222 623
Sunaway Motel – (02) 6685 3369
Tallow Beach Motel – (02) 6685 3369
The Park Hotel Motel – (02) 6685 3641; (02) 6685 3222
Wollongbar Motor Inn – (02) 6685 8200

Agencies
WORKDIRECTIONS AUSTRALIA – (02) 6639 7777
ON-Q HUMAN – (02) 6685 5733

Nursing
Agencies
For nursing positions in hospitals in Byron Bay and the surrounding area, get in touch with the agencies below, based in Sydney:
CAMPAIGN NURSING – (02) 9241 3675
DIAL A NURSE – (02) 9572 9311
DRAKE MEDOX – (02) 9273 0501

GORDON NURSES – (02) 9953 9388
ID MEDICAL STAFFING – (02) 9957 1166
MEDICAL RECRUITMENT – (02) 9232 0700
MEDISTAFF – 1800 676 856
NURSING EXCELLENCE – (02) 9552 3975

You will need to register as a nurse at:
New South Wales State Nursing Registration Board, PO Box K599,
Haymarket, NSW 2001
Tel: (02) 9219 0222
nursesreg@doh.health.nsw.gov.au

For more information contact:
State Government Overseas Qualifications Unit
Qualifications Officer, Ground Floor, 255 Elizabeth Street, Sydney
NSW 2000
Tel: (02) 9269 3500

Teaching
Agencies
For teaching positions in Byron Bay and the surrounding area, get in
touch with the agencies below, based in Sydney:
DRAKE OVERLOAD – (02) 9273 0500
SELECT EDUCATION – (02) 8258 9800
TIMEPLAN – (02) 9838 0148

Independent schools
Association of Independent Schools New South Wales
Tel: (02) 9299 2845
    Contact individual employers for vacancies in independent schools
in New South Wales.

For information on registering as a teacher in New South Wales:
www.schools.nsw.edu.au – New South Wales Education Authority

Support

Internet cafes
Koo Kafe Marvel Street – (02) 6685 5711
*Internet Outpost@Soundwave*s 58 Jonson Street – (02) 6680 7986
Global Gossip Byron Bay 84 Jonson Street – (02) 6680 9140

Byron Bus & Backpacker Centre
84 Jonson Street, Byron Bay
Tel: (02) 6685 5517
Open Mon-Fri 7.30am-7pm; Sat-Sun 8am-7pm

Visitor Information Centre
Stationmaster's Cottage, 80 Jonson Street, Byron Bay
Tel: (02) 6680 8558
Fax: (02) 6685 5351
Email: *info@visitbyronbay.com*
www.visitbyronbay.com
Open 9am-5pm daily

Banks
ANZ – Byron Bay, 57 Jonson Street, NSW 2481
Westpac – Byron Bay, 73 Jonson Street, NSW 2481

Hospitals
Byron District Hospital, Wordsworth Street – (02) 6685 6200

If you are a victim of crime or need community advice:
Byron Bay Police Station
Headquarters – Byron Bay Police, 20 Shirley Street, Byron Bay
Tel: (02) 6685 9499
Tel: 131444 for non-emergency
Tel: 000 Emergency

Cool places to hang out...

- The beach! Catch some rays, and generally relax and enjoy yourself on some of Australia's best beaches.
- The sea – from surfing to sea-kayaking and scuba diving, Byron Bay is a mecca for fans of all things watery.

Things to do in Byron Bay...

- Surf! Byron Bay is world famous for its immaculate beaches and great surfing.
- Go hiking – walking trips into the bush are a great way to see some of Australia's most stunning national parks.
- Head to the East Coast Blues and Roots Festival in Easter or one of the many other great festivals that Byron Bay attracts.

TOWN BY TOWN

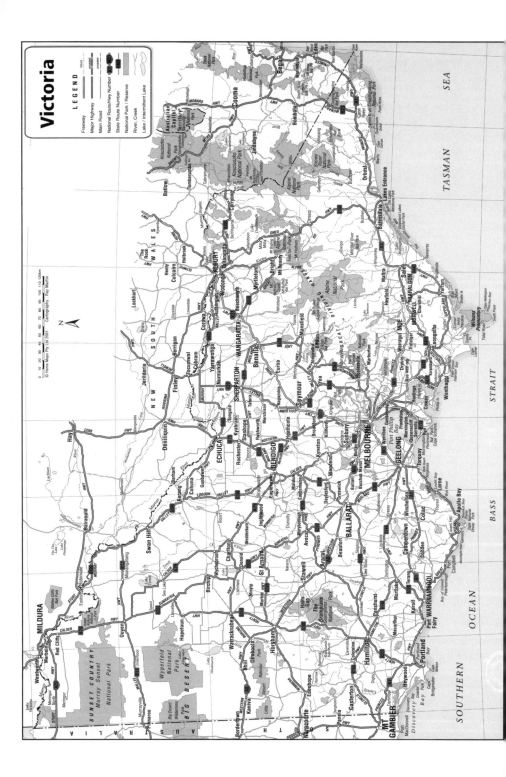

Victoria

One of the best things about Victoria is that it contains not only Melbourne, one of Australia's hippest and most loveable cities, but also the Yarra Valley, home to some of Australia's finest wines. Melbourne is a great city to hang out in, with plenty of work available to working holidaymakers, as well as plenty of seasonal work available in the wine-growing regions. Victoria is a great place to head to if you enjoy the great outdoors, and Melbourne's many arts events and music festivals make it a must for all culture vultures.

....

Melbourne

Why Melbourne?

It's a city where art and sport rubs shoulders, where you'll find fantastic food and even better shopping. It is a city that provides a great base for visiting the rest of Victoria, but which also rewards anyone who wants to stay and discover its many pleasures. It's a hip and avant-garde city, and a great place to discover the things that make Australia the great country it is – frankness, open-mindedness and an enthusiasm for the good life in one of the world's great cosmopolitan cities.

SOME MELBOURNE FACTS
▶ Since 1966 it's been illegal to harness a dog and force it to drive a vehicle in Melbourne.
▶ 1966 was a bad year – it also became illegal to have an article of disguise with you without a good excuse.

Getting to and around Melbourne

Taxi: Taxis are available at the airport from the ground floor level of the terminal building, in front of the South Terminal and the Qantas Terminal and take about 30 minutes into the city centre.

Bus: SkyBus (tel: (03) 9335 2811; website: *www.skybus.com.au*) operates daily 24 hours between the airport and the city centre. Information on destinations served and schedules is available from the information desks in the terminal building.

Accommodation

Rentals
Peter Markovic Real Estate
Fitzroy Office, 109 Smith Street, Fitzroy, VIC 3065
Tel: (03) 9419 5555
Email: *rentals@petermarkovic.com.au*
Website: *www.petermarkovic.com.au*

Heritage Property Group
474 St Kilda Street, Melbourne, VIC 3004
Tel: (03) 9869 1000
Email: *info@hpgonline.com.au*
Website: *www.hpgonline.com.au*

USEFUL INFO
► To call Melbourne from the UK or Ireland dial 0061 + 3 + eight digit number.

TOWN BY TOWN

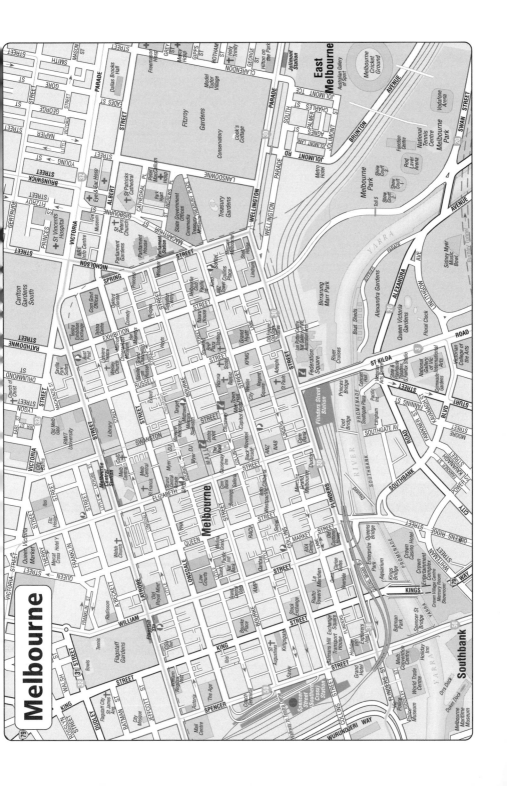

Hostels
Central
City Central 475 Spencer Street – (03) 9329 7725
Elizabeth Hostel 490 Elizabeth Street – (03) 9663 1685
Flinders Station Backpackers 35 Elizabeth Street – (03) 9620 5100
Hotel Bakpak 167 Franklin Street – Freecall 1800 645 200
Toad Hall 441 Elizabeth Street – (03) 9600 9010

Fitzroy/East Melbourne
East Melbourne Hotel 2 Hotham Street – (03) 9419 2040
The Nunnery 116 Nicholson Street Fitzroy – 1800 032 635

North Melbourne
Bev & Mick's 312 Victoria Street – (03) 9329 7156
Chapman Gardens 76 Chapman Street – (03) 9328 3595
Global Backpackers 238 Victoria Street – (03) 9328 3728

Saint Kilda
Enfield House 2 Enfield Street – (03) 9534 8159
Jackson's Manor 53 Jackson Street – (03) 9534 1877
Oslo Hotel 38 Grey Street – (03) 9525 4498
St Kilda Lodge 79 Grey Street – (03) 9525 4054

HOTEL BAKPAK

Abandon all thoughts of roughing it in youth hostels – Australian hostels have come a long way in recent years. A fine example of this is the Hotel Bakpak in Melbourne, which has an in-house employment agency, a café, cinema, lounge area, and its own backpacker bar featuring DJs and live bands. You even get free entry into a local gym! The Bakpak group runs a handful of hostels along the east coast, all of which have a high standard of facilities. For more info, go to *www.bakpakgroup.com.*

Windsor

Nomads Chapel St 22 Chapel Street – (03) 9533 6855
Nomads Pint on Punt 42 Punt Road – (03) 9510 4273
Queensberry YHA 78 Howard Street North – (03) 9329 8599

Work

Harvest work in Victoria

Below are a few places where it's possible to get a job fruit picking in Victoria, along with all the best times to go and how far away they are from the major cities. For a more expansive list, visit *www.jobsearch.gov.au/harvesttrail/* where jobs are listed and frequently updated, and you can also get information galore on each town.

Beechworth

About three hours from Melbourne and roughly seven hours from Sydney, Beechworth is the Outback at its best.
February to April – *grape picking*
March to May – *apples*
June to August – *grape pruning*
November to December – *cherries*

Shepparton

Only two hours drive from Melbourne, with towns such as Bunbartha, Cobram, Echuca and Grahamvale all a very short distance away.
November to March – *stone fruits*
February to June – *soft fruits*
July to April – *citrus fruits*
January to February – *vegetables*

Office work

ADECCO – (03) 9920 4100
CATALYST – (03) 9699 1055

CENTASTAFF – (03) 9330 4566
DLA – (03) 9670 4244
DRAKE – (03) 9245 0200
HOBAN – (03) 92(03) 4900
IPA – (03) 9252 2222
JULIA ROSS – (03) 96(02) 5550
LINK – (03) 96(08) 6222
REDDIN – (03) 9672 6700
WESTAFF – (03) 9699 3544

Accountancy
ACCOUNTANCY LINK – (03) 96(08) 6222
ACCOUNTANCY OPTIONS – (03) 9620 9600
BALANCE – (03) 9621 1999
JONATHAN WREN – (03) 9963 6300
MICHAEL PAGE – (03) 96(07) 5600
MORGAN BANKS – (03) 9623 6666
ROBERT HALF – (03) 9691 3631

IT
AUSTRALIA WIDE IT – (03) 9321 0109
CANDLE IT – (03) 9832 8000
DRAKE – (03) 9631 6111
HAYS IT – (03) 9614 7677
MICHAEL PAGE – (03) 96(07) 5600
TCS COMPUTERSTAFF – (03) 9818 0034

Hospitality employers
Bars that may employ travellers with Working Holiday Makers (WHM) visas
Arizona Bar 127 Russell Street – (03) 9654 5000
Builders Arms 211 Gertrude Street – (03) 9419 0818
Box 189 Collins Street – (03) 9663 0411
Match Bar 58 Bull Street – (03) 5441 4403

Melbourne Metro 20-30 Bourke Street – (03) 9662 3798
Molly Blooms 39 Bay Street – (03) 9646 2681
Studio 54 2 Queen Street – (03) 5441 8711
PJ O'Briens Ground Floor, Southgate Arts & Leisure Precinct, Southbank – (03) 9686 5011
The Public Bar 238 Victoria Street North – (03) 9329 6522
Places Restaurant and Bar 24 Little Bourke Street – (03) 9665 2666

Melbourne hotels that may employ travellers on WHM visas
All Seasons Welcome Hotel 265 Little Bourke Street – (03) 9639 0555
Rainbow Hotel 27 St David Street Fitzroy – (03) 9419 4193
Windsor Hotel 1(03) Spring Street – (03) 9633 6000

Agencies
PINNACLE HOSPITALITY – (03) 9620 9666
SKILLED PERSONNEL – (03) 9924 2424

Nursing
Agencies
ANS – (03) 9662 9922

BMG – (03) 9416 2333/1800 677 948
DRAKE MEDOX – 1300 360 070
MEDISTAFF – (03) 9510 1444
OXLEY – 1300 360456

You will need to register as a nurse at:
Nurses Board of Victoria, PO Box 4932, Melbourne –
Tel: (03) 8635 1200

Teaching
Agencies
BMG – (03) 9416 2333/1800 677 948 (recruits teachers and nurses)
SELECT – (03) 8663 4755

You will need to register as a teacher at:
www.sofweb.vic.edu.au – Victoria Education Authority (for government schools)
... or *www.sofweb.vic.edu.au/rsb* – The Registered Schools Board for non-government schools

For more information, go to:
Overseas Qualifications Unit, Level 27, Nauru House, 80 Collins Street, Melbourne – (03) 9655 6164

Support

Internet cafes
Cafe Wired 363 Clarendon Street, South Melbourne – (03) 9686 9555
Cyber Chat 181-189 Barkly, St Kilda- (03) 9534 0859
Cyberia St Kilda 9 Grey Street, St Kilda – (03) 9534 2666
Melbourne Central Internet 133 Melbourne Central – (03) 9663 8410
Outlook 196 Commercial Road, Prahran – (03) 9521 4227

PAUL LEWIS, 24

Initially, my gap year was taken so I could go and play cricket for Fremantle, Perth. After three months of doing so I was running out of money. I needed a job, badly! Luckily, finding one was simple. The local rag came good, advertizing a vacancy for 'Lettuce Engineers'.

Two days later I started as a lettuce cutter (I mean lettuce engineer). The company supplied salads for Quantas Airlines and I was part of a production line consisting of people from literally everywhere. To my left, a pretty Perth girl, to my right a mad South African guy, and opposite a very chirpy German... the list goes on.

Despite starting work at 4am, working in giant fridges and cleaning up rotten vegetables, I was having the time of my life. We finished at 12 and went straight to the beach to sunbathe, swim and sleep!

After three months of hard work, myself and some fellow 'Lettuce

Engineers' decided to take our bronzed bodies eastwards to explore some more of Australia's delights. We climbed Ayers Rock, camped at Alice Springs and eventually stumbled into Cairns. Here we bought a camper van and made our way to Sydney.

Three months later, we arrived in Sydney, even browner! I had sky dived over the Whitsunday Islands, dived on the barrier reef, spent a week on a sailing yacht and drank enough alcohol to last me a lifetime (or so I thought).

We all managed to find work in Sydney. I sold telephones, the chirpy German laboured for a building farm, the mad South African worked in a bar... oh, and the pretty Perth girl that we dragged along with us sold tickets at the Grand Opera house!

We all remain friends to this day and have met since in Amsterdam of all places. To conclude, we all worked in Australia and Australia certainly worked for us!

Backpackers World
440 Elizabeth Street – (03) 9662 4666

Student Uni Travel
440 Elizabeth Street – (03) 9662 4666

Travellers Aid
169 Swanston Street – (03) 9654 2600

YHA Travel
205 King Street – (03) 9670 9611

Banks
ANZ – 254 Queen Street – 131314
Commonwealth – 21 Swanston Street, Melbourne

Hospitals
Royal Melbourne, Poplar Road, Parkville – (03) 9387 2211

If you are a victim of crime or need community advice:
Victoria Police Centre
637 Flinders Street, Melbourne, Victoria 3005
Tel: 000 Emergency

Cool places to hang out...
Builders Arms 211 Gertrude Street, Fitzroy – (03) 9419 0818
Chevron Club 519 St Kilda Road – (03) 9510 1281
Club UK 169 Exhibition Street – Carwash Disco on Wednesdays –
    (03) 9663 2075
Esplanade (Espy) 11 Upper Esplanade, St Kilda – (03) 9534 0211
Great Britain Hotel 447 Church Street, Richmond – (03) 9429 5066
Hairy Canary 212 Little Collins Street – (03) 9654 2471
Melbourne Metro 20 Bourke Street – (03) 9663 4288
Pint on Punt 42 Punt Road, Windsor – (03) 9510 4273

Prince Of Wales 29 Fitzroy Street, St Kilda – (03) 9536 1168
Roo Bar Hotel Bak Pak 167 Franklin Street – (03) 9329 7525

Things to do in Melbourne...

- See the Melbourne Aquarium.
- Go to The National Gallery of Victoria.
- Check out the Victoria Arts Centre (next to the National Gallery on St Kilda Road).
- Take a trip to the high country for the snow (July and August).
- Browse the Queen Victoria Market (corner of Elizabeth and Victoria Streets) and the Victorian Arts Centre Market, 100 St Kilda Road, on a Sunday.
- Take a tipsy day trip and explore the wineries of the Yarra valley.
- Visit the Dandenong Ranges for the rainforests.
- See the penguin parade at Philip Island (*www.penguinislandtour.com.au*).

And if you're into sport...

- AFL Season (July-September).
- The Grand Prix (February-March).
- Australian Tennis Open (January).
- The Melbourne Cup (November).

These are also good times to look for hospitality and catering temp work.

Visitor Information Centre:

Corner Flinders Street and St Kilda Road, Melbourne, Victoria 3000
Tel: (03) 9658 9658; (03) 9650 6168

Geelong

Why Geelong?
Geelong is the second largest city in Victoria (after Melbourne). It's a big, busy place that's well worth staying in for a while – there's plenty of work and it's a good base for the surrounding area.

SOME GEELONG FACTS
► Geelong has a great music scene – make sure you check out some bands.
► Geelong is close to the stunning Great Ocean Road – don't miss it!

Accommodation

Rentals
Castle Real Estate
110a Pakington Street, Geelong West 3218
Tel: (03) 5222 5228
Fax: (03) 5222 3131
Email: *rentals@castle.com.au*

Barry Plant Doherty
Shop 1, 230 Moorabool Street, Geelong, Victoria 3220
Tel: (03) 5221 4011
Website: *www.barryplantdoherty.com.au*

Hostels
Nomads National Hotel 191 Moorabool Street, Geelong –
    (03) 5229 1211
Irish Murphys 30 Aberdeen Street, Geelong – (03) 5222 2900

Work

Office work

ADECCO GEELONG – (03) 5228 5000

ALPHA OMEGA CONSULTING GROUP NORTH GEELONG – (03) 5278 9123

CENTACARE EMPLOYMENT GEELONG – (03) 5221 7055

DIRECT RECRUITMENT GEELONG – (03) 5221 3880

GEELONG EMPLOY ABILITY – (03) 5222 3377

IPA PERSONNEL GEELONG – (03) 5225 3999

JK PERSONNEL GEELONG – (03) 5249 4000

JOB FUTURES GEELONG WEST – (03) 5221 6160

JOBS A NEW APPROACH GEELONG – (03) 5222 8000

MATCHWORKS GEELONG – (03) 5229 7250

MEGT GEELONG – (03) 5222 6906

PEOPLE AT WORK GEELONG – (03) 5221 5599

SKILLED ENGINEERING GEELONG NORTH – (03) 5278 8944

SUPPORTWORKS GEELONG – (03) 5229 0222

VITALITY PERSONNEL GEELONG – (03) 5222 8585

Accountancy

ADECCO GEELONG – (03) 5228 5000

IT

ADECCO GEELONG – (03) 5228 5000

CENTACARE EMPLOYMENT GEELONG – (03) 5221 7055

Hospitality employers
Bars that may employ travellers with Working Holiday Makers (WHM) visas
My Place 40 Moorabool Street – (03) 5223 2944
Planet Pool 50 Little Ryrie Street – (03) 5223 2911
Statik Bar & Lounge – (03) 5222 1008
Venom Nightclub 5 James Street – (03) 5222 5025
The Wool Exchange Nightclub 44 Corio Street – (03) 5224 2400

Geelong hotels that may employ travellers on WHM visas
Best Western Geelong Motor Inn & Serviced Apartments Corner of
     Princes Highway and Kooyong Road – (03) 5222 4777
Comfort Inn Eastern Sands 1 Bellerine Street – (03) 5221 5577
Comfort Inn Parkside 68 High Street, Belmont – (03) 5243 6766
Four Points By Sheraton 10-14 Eastern Beach Road – (03) 5223 1377
Mercure Hotel Geelong Corner of Gheringhap Street and Myers Street –
     (03) 5223 6200
Sundowner Geelong 13 The Esplanade – (03) 5244 7700

Agencies
ADECCO GEELONG – (03) 5228 5000
CENTACARE EMPLOYMENT GEELONG – (03) 5221 7055

Nursing
Agencies in Geelong
CENTACARE EMPLOYMENT GEELONG – (03) 5221 7055

Alternatively, try the agencies below, based in Melbourne:
ANS – (03) 9662 9922
BMG – (03) 9416 2333/1800 677 948
DRAKE MEDOX – 1300 360 070
MEDISTAFF – (03) 9510 1444
OXLEY – 1300 360456

You will need to register as a nurse at:
Nurses Board of Victoria, PO Box 4932, Melbourne –
Tel: (03) 8635 1200

Teaching
Agencies in Geelong
ADECCO GEELONG – (03) 5228 5000
CENTACARE EMPLOYMENT GEELONG – (03) 5221 7055

Also try the following agencies based in Melbourne –
BMG – (03) 9416 2333/1800 677 948 (recruits teachers and nurses)
SELECT – (03) 8663 4755

You will need to register as a teacher at:
www.sofweb.vic.edu.au – Victoria Education Authority (for government
schools)
... or *www.sofweb.vic.edu.au/rsb* – The Registered Schools Board for
non-government schools

For more information, go to:
Overseas Qualifications Unit, Level 27, Nauru House, 80 Collins Street,
Melbourne – (03) 9655 6164

Support

Internet cafes
Australian Red Centre Adventures, Geelong, PO Box 361, Geelong North
Tel: (03) 5277 0870

Geelong and Great Ocean Road Visitor Information Centre
Stead Park, Princes Highway, Corio – (03) 5275 5797 or 1800 620 888
Open 9am-5pm daily

Geelong Visitor Information Centre

National Wool Museum, corner of Moorabool Street and
Brougham Street
Tel: (03) 5222 2900 or 1800 620 888
Open 9am-5pm daily

Banks

ANZ – 83 Malop Street, Geelong, Victoria 3220
Westpac – 95-97 Moorabool Street, Geelong, Victoria 3220

Hospitals

The Geelong Hospital, Ryrie Street – (03) 5226 7111

If you are a victim of crime or need community advice:

Geelong Police
Level 5, 30-38 Little Malop Street
Tel: (03) 5223 7800.
Tel: 131444 for non-emergency
Tel: 000 Emergency

Cool places to hang out...

- Some great surfing beaches at Torquay and Jan Juc.
- Geelong's fabulous Sunday Markets.

Things to do in Geelong...

- Head to the National Wool Museum – it's more interesting than it sounds!
- Chill out on the waterfront.
- Shop till you drop at Geelong's Sunday Markets.
- Head out of town and go horse riding on the beach at Sorrento.

Queensland

When people think of Australia, they think of many of Queensland's greatest attractions. It's hard to argue with a state that contains the Great Barrier Reef, rainforests and some of the finest surfing beaches on the planet. If you get a job there and manage to stay for a bit longer, there are also opportunities to go whale-watching, bungee-jumping and to pack in as many adrenaline-fuelled activities as your body can handle.

Brisbane

Why Brisbane?

The capital of Queensland makes a great base to explore this stunning area – and the city itself has plenty to keep you occupied if you plan to spend a bit longer here. From the stunning views from Mt Coot-Tha to the city's buzzing restaurants and markets, there's something for everyone. It's also a great place to stay if you want to explore the Gold and Sunshine Coasts – just bear in mind that many South Australians head north to escape the freezing winters of the Southern Hemisphere, so it does get busy!

SOME BRISBANE FACTS
► The box jellyfish, found off the coast of Queensland, can kill you in three minutes.
► You're still allowed to cuddle Koalas in Queensland, but only up to 30 minutes per day.

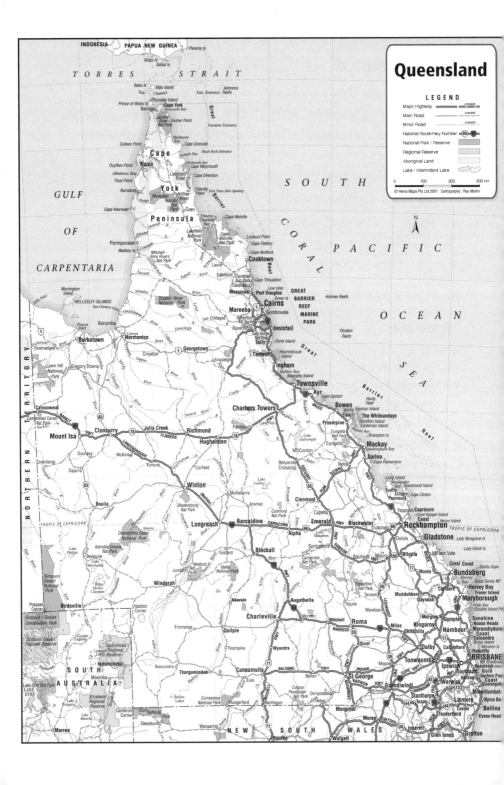

Getting to and around Brisbane

Rail: The Airtrain (tel: (07) 3216 3308; website: *www.airtrain.com.au*) provides services to Brisbane Central Station (journey time: 22 minutes) and to the Gold Coast. Airtrain stations are located directly outside the Domestic and International terminals.

Taxi: Taxis are always available. Companies include Black & White Cabs (tel: 131998; website: *www.blackandwhitecabs.com.au*) and Yellow Cabs (tel: 132227 or (07) 3391 5955; website: *www.yellowcab.com.au*).

Bus: Airport buses are available from both terminals to Brisbane Transit Centre in Roma Street, the Gold Coast and the Sunshine Coast. A door-to-door service is also provided. For further information, contact Coachtrans (tel: (07) 3238 4700; website: *www.coachtrans.com.au*).

Visitor Information Centre:
Brisbane Visitor Information Centre
Corner Albert and Queen Streets, Brisbane City, Brisbane,
Queensland 4002 – (07) 3006 6290
Email: *jerrington@brisbanemarketing.com.au*
Website: *www.ourbrisbane.com*

TOWN BY TOWN

USEFUL INFO
▶ To call Brisbane from the UK and Ireland, dial 0061 + 7 + eight digit number.

Accommodation

Rentals
L.J. Hooker City Residential
Level 1, 293 Queen Street
Tel: (07) 3232 5888
Fax: (07) 3232 5822
Email: *cityresbrisbane@ljh.com.au*
Website: *www.ljhooker.com.au/cityresbrisbane*

Harcourts City Sales & Rentals
60 Leichhardt Street, Spring Hill, Brisbane, Queensland
Tel: (07) 3839-5000
Fax: (07) 3839-5003
Email: *harcourts@innerbrisbane.com*
Website: *www.innerbrisbane.com*

Hostels
The City
Aussie Way Backpackers 34 Cricket Street – (07) 3369 0711
Banana Bender 118 Petrie Terrace – (07) 3367 1157
Brisbane City YHA 392 Upper Roma Street – (07) 3236 1004
City Backpackers Upper Roma Street – (07) 3211 3221
Palace Backpackers (above Downunder Bar) Corner of Ann Street and
     Edward Street – (07) 3211 2433
Yellow Submarine 66 Quay Street – (07) 3211 3424

Fortitude Valley
Balmoral House 33 Amelia Street – (07) 3252 1397
Home for Backpackers 515 Brunswick Street – (07) 3254 1984
Reefo 14-20 Constance Street – 1800 173336
Shamrock Hotel 186 Brunswick Street – (07) 3252 2421

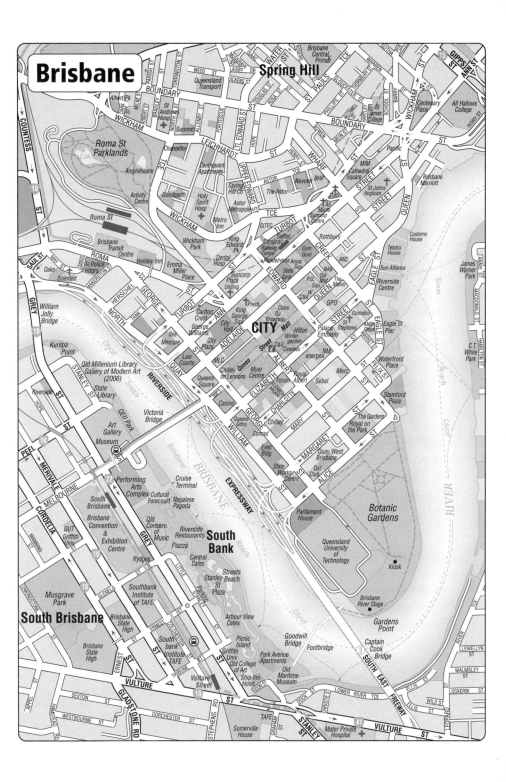

New Farm
Bowen Terrace 365 Bowen Terrace – (07) 3254 0458
Brisbane Homestead 57 Annie Street – (07) 3358 3538
Globetrekkers 35 Balfour Street – (07) 3358 1251
Pete's Palace 515 Brunswick Street – (07) 3254 1984

West End (south of river)
Brisbane Backpackers Resort 110 Vulture Street – 1800 626 452
Somewhere To Stay 45 Brighton Road – (07) 3846 2858

Work

Harvest work in Queensland
Below are a few places where it's possible to get a job fruit picking
in Queensland, along with all the best times to go and how far away
they are from the major cities. For a more expansive list, visit
www.jobsearch.gov.au/harvesttrail/ where jobs are listed and frequently
updated and you can get information galore on each town.

Atherton
Atherton is 94km inland to the south west of Cairns in the Tablelands
area of Far North Queensland.
February to July – *avocados*
January to December – *bananas*
January to December – *citrus fruits*
January to December – *potatoes*

Bundaberg
Bundaberg is 360km north of Brisbane. It is on the Burnett River and
14km from the coast. It is a city in the sub-tropics where the rainfall is
considerable and the average daily summer temperatures vary between
20 and 30 degrees.
March to July – *citrus fruits*

April to July – *vegetables*
April to August – *capsicums*
April to August – *rockmelons*
April to August – *zucchini*
September to December – *vegetables*
October to January – *tomatoes*
December to February – *tropical fruits and mangoes*

Office work
ADECCO – 132993/(07) 3000 1500
CATALYST – (07) 3272 9466
DRAKE – 131448
HAYS PERSONNEL – (07) 3243 3099
IPA – (07) 3225 7500
KELLY – (07) 3234 3333
MANPOWER – 132502
READY – (07) 3255 2870/(07) 3210 2039
RECRUITMENT SOLUTIONS – (07) 3221 1366
SELECT – (07) 3243 3900

Accountancy
BALANCE ACCOUNTANCY PROFESSIONALS – (07) 3229 7455
KPMG – (07) 3233 3111
MERITUS – (07) 3243 3933

IT
AMBIT – (07) 3845 7570
DIVERSITI – (07) 3210 4444
DRAKE IT – (07) 3291 6099
HAYS – (07) 3839 5044

Hospitality employers
Bars that may employ travellers with Working Holiday Makers (WHM) visas

Hotel Carindale Carindale Street, Carindale – (07) 3395 0122; 15 mins from the city, this hotel also has three bars/restaurants: *Bakers Grill Restaurant & Bar*, *Finn MacCool's Irish Bar* and *Starclub Pokies Gaming Lounge*

Adrenalin Sports Café 127 Charlotte Street – (07) 3229 1515

Casablanca 52 Petrie Terrace – (07) 3369 6969

Downunder Bar 308 Edward Street, Brisbane – (07) 3211 9277

Hotel LA Petrie Terrace – (07) 3368 2560

Someplace Else 249 Turbot Street – (07) 3835 3535

Brisbane hotels that may employ travellers with WHM visas

Couran Cove Resort HR Dept, PO Box 224, Runaway Bay, QLD 4216 You can fax them on (07) 5597 9090 or call free in Australia on 1800 268726

Quay West Suites 132 Alice Street – (07) 3853 6000

The Carlton Crest Hotel King George Square – (07) 3229 9111

Agencies

CATALYST – (07) 3218 2710

CORDON BLEU PERSONNEL – (07) 3221 1722

FIRST HOSPITALITY – (07) 3257 1844

PINNACLE – (07) 3220 3244

QUEENSLAND HOSPITALITY & SECURITY STAFF – (07) 3257 0020

ZENITH HOSPITALITY – (07) 3831 4511

Nursing
Agencies

CRITIQUE NURSES – (07) 3341 3999

HEALTHSTRA – 131148

OXLEY NURSING – (07) 3222 4800

QUEENSLAND NURSING AGENCY – (07) 3221 9883

You will need to register as a nurse at:
Queensland Nursing Council, GPO Box 2928, Brisbane
Tel: (07) 3223 5110

Teaching
Agencies
DRAKE – (07) 3291 6099

Recognition of overseas qualifications
You should first contact the department that deals with recognition
of overseas qualifications, before you can register as a teacher in
Queensland.

Skills Recognition Branch, Level 5, Education House, 30 Mary Street,
Brisbane, Queensland 4000 – (07) 3234 9900
www.trainandemploy.qld.gov.au

Registering as a teacher
In Queensland there are two different boards of teacher registration
depending on whether you wish to work solely in government or public
sector schools, or in both public and private schools. You will need to
register as a teacher at:
www.education.qld.gov.au – Queensland Education Authority (for
government schools)
www.btr.qld.edu.au – Board of Teacher Registration for all schools

Support

Internet cafes
Dialup Cyber Lounge 126 Adelaide Street – (07) 3211 9095
Email Plus 328 Upper Roma Street – (07) 3236 0433
Grand Orbit Shop 16/17 Level 1, Eagle Street Pier – (07) 3236 1384
The Hub 125 Margaret Street – (07) 3229 1119

Backpackers Travel Centre
138 Albert Street – (07) 3221 2225

Centrepoint Backpackers Employment & Accommodation Service
1005 Ann Street – 1800 06 1522

Student Uni Travel
201 Elizabeth Street – (07) 3003 0344

YHA Travel
154 Roma Street – (07) 3236 1680

Banks
ANZ – 324 Queen Street
Commonwealth – 240 Queen Street – (07) 3237 3067

Hospitals
Royal Brisbane, Herston Road – (07) 3253 8111

If you are a victim of crime or need community advice:
Police Headquarters
200 Roma Street, Brisbane, Queensland 4000
Tel: (07) 3364 6464
Tel: 000 Emergency

Cool places to hang out...
Brunswick Hotel 569 Brunswick Street, New Farm – (07) 3358 1181
Downunder Bar 3(08) Edward Street – (07) 3211 9277
Empire Hotel 339 Brunswick Street – (07) 3852 1216

Fortitude Valley is an area of Brisbane with a reputation for excellent nightclubs and alternative bars.
Ric's Café 321 Brunswick Street – (07) 3854 1772

Shamrock Hotel 186 Brunswick Street – (07) 3252 2421
Storybridge Hotel 200 Main Street, Kangaroo Point – (07) 3391 2266

Things to do in Brisbane...

- Visit Southbank Parklands for 'Australia's only inland inner city beach', restaurants and markets.
- Go all gooey over the Koalas at the Lone Pine Koala Sanctuary.
- Explore the Queensland Museum in the Queensland Cultural Centre.
- Mt Coot-Tha Botanic Gardens are a good place to chill out and enjoy the views.
- The Gold Coast (to the South) and the Sunshine Coast (to the North) are only an hour's drive from Brisbane. The stunning beaches and scenery make this part of Queensland one of the most popular destinations in Australia. Resorts along both coasts get extremely busy during school holidays.
- Moreton Bay island is a good option if you want to get away from the hustle and bustle of the Gold and Sunshine coast resorts.
- Take the passenger ferry from the city for a sun seeking day trip.
- St Helena island has the remains of a colonial prison to explore.
- 90 minutes from Brisbane is the Tangalooma Wild Dolphin Resort, where you can whale and dolphin watch.
- Queensland has a multitude of theme parks to visit, from the wet and the wonderful to the downright weird.
  Gold Coast Dreamworld Coomera – (07) 5588 1111
  Seaworld Main Beach – (07) 5588 2205
  Warner Brothers Movie World Pacific Highway Oxenford – (07) 5573 8485
  Wet 'n' Wild Pacific Highway, Oxenford – (07) 5573 2277
  Underwater World Mooloolaba – (07) 5444 2255

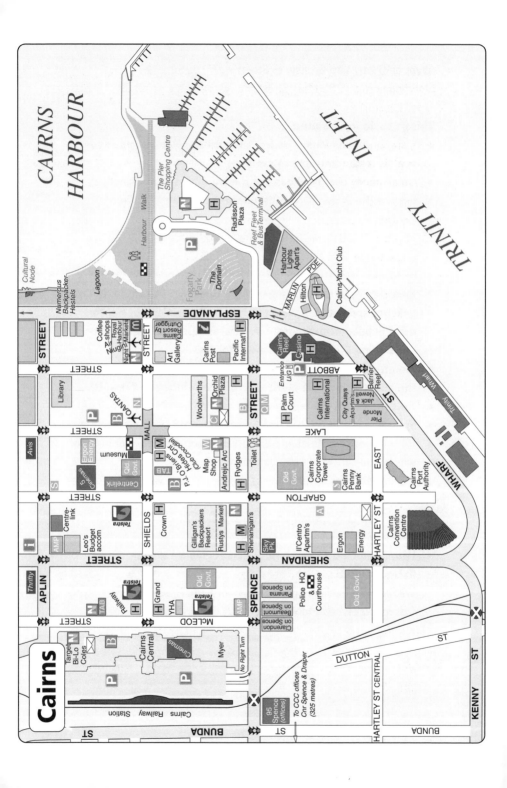

Cairns

Why Cairns?

Cairns is a cool place to hang out for a while, and there are plenty of bars and restaurants to keep you busy while you're planning your next adventure. And that is what Cairns is really all about for most of its visitors – it's a place to arrange your trip out to the Great Barrier Reef or to some many of the beautiful islands that lie off the Queensland coast. Cairns has got a lively nightlife and certainly makes a great base from which to visit some of Oz's most spectacular sights. Cairns is hugely popular with backpackers, as it is within striking distance of the Great Barrier Reef and the rainforests of the Cape York Peninsula. If adrenalin is your thing, then there's plenty of opportunity to get your fix with activities ranging from bungee jumping to white-water rafting.

SOME CAIRNS FACTS
► Babinda Boulders, south of Cairns, has a haunted pool that will kill any unmarried man who swims there!
► It's a great place to view sharks. Just little ones...

Getting to and around Cairns

Bus: Australia Coach operates an airport shuttle bus service to hotels and the city centre – fare $8 per person. Sun Palm Express Coaches operate services to the Northern Beaches, Palm Cove, Port Douglas and Cape Tribulation. Both companies pick up immediately in front of the arrivals area at both terminals and both operate an information desk within the terminal, which, if not staffed, have direct-dial telephone.

Taxi: The taxi ranks are immediately outside the airport, with the average fare to the city being $15.

Accommodation

Rentals
L.J. Hooker Cairns South
Shop 1, 494 Mulgrave Road
Tel: (07) 4033 1366
Fax: (07) 4033 1516
Email: *cairnssouth@ljh.com.au*
Website: *www.ljhooker.com.au/cairnssouth*

Ray White Central Real Estate
12a Aplin Street, Cairns 4870
Tel: (07) 4051 0555
Email: *central.qld@raywhite.com*
Website: *www.raywhite.com*

Hostels
Bel Air By The Sea 155 Esplanade, Cairns – (07) 4031 4790
Dreamtime Travellers Rest 4 Terminus Street, Cairns – (07) 4031 6753
Sunny Grove 42 Grove Street, Cairns – (07) 4051 4513
Tropic Days 26-28 Bunting Street, Cairns – (07) 4041 1521
Hollys Hostel 72 Abbott Street, Cairns – (07) 4031 1788
Tracks Hostel Backpackers 149 Grafton Street, Cairns – (07) 4031 1474
The Big Back Yard Hostel 34 Martyn Street, Cairns – (07) 4031 3133
Tropic Days Backpackers 26 Bunting Street, Cairns – (07) 4041 1521
Central City Backpackers 72 Grafton Street, Carins – (07) 4041 6511
Cairns Backpackers Inn 242 Grafton Street, Cairns – (07) 4051 9166
Travellers Castle 209 Lake Street, Cairns – (07) 40312229
Hostel 89 89 The Esplanade, Cairns – 1800 061712

USEFUL INFO
► To call Cairns from the UK ring 0061 + 7 + eight digit number.

JJ's Backpackers 11 Charles Street, Cairns – (07) 4051 7642
Cairns Girls Hostel 147 Lake Street, Cairns – (07) 4051 2016
Travellers Oasis 8 Scott Street, Cairns – 1800 621353
The McLeod Street YHA 20-24 McLeod Street, Cairns – (07) 4051 0772
Caravella's Backpackers 77 The Esplanade, Cairns – (07) 4051 2159
Jimmy's on the Esplanade 83 The Esplanade, Cairns – (07) 4031 6884
Bellview The Esplanade, Cairns – (07) 40314377
Billabong Backpackers 69 Spence Street, Cairns – (07) 4051 6946

Work

Office work
CENTACARE – (07) 4052 8000
ADECCO – (07) 4048 7300
SIGNATURE STAFF – (07) 4050 3888
BLACK & WHITE BRIGADE – (07) 4031 1128
SKILLED – 1300 366 606
PRERECRUITMENT – (07) 4031 8388
OXLEY NURSING SERVICE PTY LTD – 1300 360 456
AUSTRALIAN JOBSEARCH – 136268
JULIA ROSS RECRUITMENT – 1300 139 922
WORKFORCE SOLUTIONS (QLD) PTY LTD – (07) 3875 0000
JOB NETWORK – 131715
SARINA RUSSO JOB ACCESS – 131559
MANPOWER – 132502
AUSTRALIAN TOURISM NETWORK – (07) 4031 2501
CHR EMPLOYMENT SERVICES – (07) 4041 5011
EMPLOYNET – (07) 4031 9494

Accountancy
CENTACARE – (07) 4052 8000
ADECCO – (07) 4048 7300
SIGNATURE STAFF – (07) 4050 3888

IT

CHR EMPLOYMENT SERVICES CAIRNS – (07) 4041 5011

Hospitality employers
Bars that may employ travellers with Working Holiday Makers (WHM) visas
The Woolshed Shields Street, Cairns – (07) 4051 8211
Cock 'n' Bull Digger Street, Cairns – (07) 4031 1160
Fox & Firkin Old English Pub Corner of Lake and Spence Street, Cairns –
    (07) 4031 5305
Willie McBrides 253 Sheridan Street, Cairns – (07) 4041 0000
Calypso Backpackers Inn 5 Digger Street, Cairns – (07) 4031 0910
The Nest Piano Bar McLeod Street, Cairns – (07) 4051 8181
The Wool Shed Char Grill & Saloon Bar City Place, Cairns (07) 4031 6304
Troppo's Non Stop Rock Corner Spence/Lake Street, Cairns (07) 4031 2530

Cairns hotels that may employ travellers on WHM visas
Pacific International Hotel 43 The Esplanade, Cairn – (07) 4051 7888
Cairns International Hotel 17 Abbott Street, Cairns – (07) 4031 1300
Oasis Resort 122 Lake Street, Cairns – (07) 4080 1888
Cairns Backpackers Inn 242 Grafton Street, Cairns
Tradewinds Esplanade Hotel 137 The Esplanade, Cairns
Calypso Backpackers Inn 5 Digger Street, Cairns – (07) 4031 0910
Pacific International Hotel 43 The Esplanade, Cairns – (07) 4051 7888

Agencies
ADECCO CAIRNS – (07) 4048 7300
CENTACARE EMPLOYMENT CAIRNS – (07) 4052 8000
SIGNATURE STAFF – (07) 4050 3888

Nursing
Agencies
ADECCO CAIRNS – (07) 4048 7300
HAYMAN ISLAND – (07) 4940 1683

CENTACARE EMPLOYMENT CAIRNS – (07) 4052 8000
NURSEWORLDWIDE CAIRNS – (07) 4031 8755

You will need to register as a nurse at:
Queensland Nursing Council
(postal) GPO Box 2928, Brisbane QLD 4001
(location) 12th Floor, Forestry House, 160 Mary Street, Brisbane
QLD 4000
Tel: (07) 3223 5160
Fax: (07) 3223 5115
Email: *registrations@qnc.qld.gov.au*
Website: *www.qnc.qld.gov.au*

Teaching
Agencies
ADECCO CAIRNS – (07) 4048 7300
CENTACARE EMPLOYMENT CAIRNS – (07) 4052 8000

Recognition of overseas qualifications
Firstly you should contact the department that deals with recognition
of overseas qualifications before you can register as a teacher in
Queensland.
Skills Recognition Branch, Level 5, Education House, 30 Mary Street,
Brisbane, Queensland 4000 – (07) 3234 9900
www.trainandemploy.qld.gov.au

Registering as a teacher
In Queensland there are two different boards of teacher registration,
depending on whether you wish to work solely in government or public
sector schools, or in both public and private schools. You will need to
register as a teacher at:
www.education.qld.gov.au – Queensland Education Authority (for
government schools)
...or *www.btr.qld.edu.au* – Board of Teacher Registration for all schools

Support

Internet Cafes
Internet Outpost Cairns at Happy Travels, 9/7 Shields Street –
(07) 4041 0666
ANN's NetCafé 1st Floor, Tropical Arcade, Corner of Abbott Street and
Shields Street
The Travellers Contact Point Clauson House, 1st Floor, 13 Shields Street,
City Place

The Queensland Government Travel Centre
Corner of Adelaide Street and Edward Street, Brisbane QLD 4000
(07) 221 6111

Travellers Contact Point
13 Shields Street, Cairns
Tel: (07) 4041 4677
www.travellers.com.au
Open 7am-midnight daily

Banks
ANZ – 21 Grafton Street, Cairns, Queensland 4870
Westpac – 63-65 Lake Street, Cairns, Queensland 4870

Hospitals
Cairns Base Hospital, The Esplanade – (07) 4050 6333

If you are a victim of crime or need community advice:
Police Headquarters
Cairns Police District Headquarters, Sheridan Street, Cairns
Tel: (07) 4030 7000
Tel: 131444 to contact nearest police station
Tel: 000 Emergency

Cool places to hang out...
- Chill out in the Flecker Botanic Gardens.
- Swim with sharks at Undersea World.

Things to do in Cairns...
- Head for the world-famous Great Barrier Reef.
- Go to Reef Teach to get a great insight into the Reef – recommended if you're planning on snorkelling on the Great Barrier Reef – *www.reefteach.com.au.*
- Spend a couple of days hiking or snorkelling on Fitzroy Island.

Cairns Visitor Centre
51 The Esplanade, Cairns – (07) 4051 3588
www.tnq.org.au
Open 8.30am-6.30pm daily

Gold Coast

Why the Gold Coast?
The Gold Coast is world famous as an area of great beaches, vibrant resorts and a fantastic climate that draws visitors from all over the world. Packed with loads of high-rise apartments, hotels, nightclubs and bars, it's also a great place to get work.

SOME GOLD COAST FACTS
- ► The aborigines used to use the area to get the wood they needed for their boomerangs.
- ► It's now Australia's largest tourist resort.

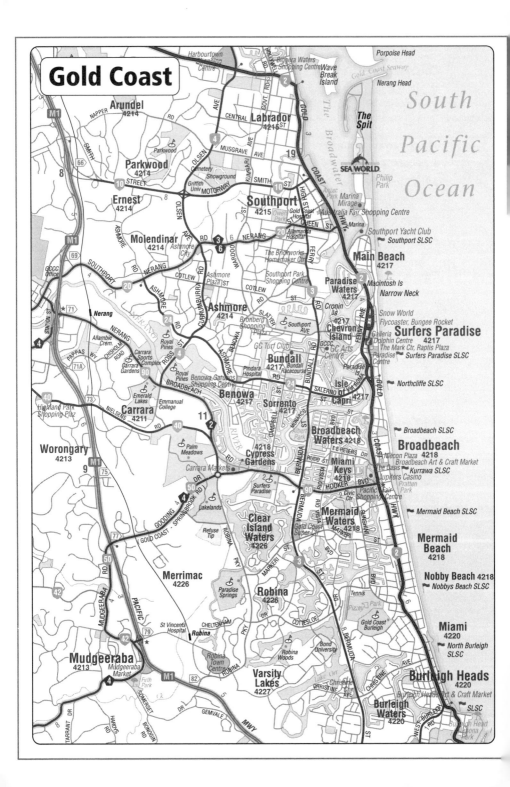

Accommodation

The place you're most likely to stay on the Gold Coast is
Surfer's Paradise:

Rentals
Harcourts Surfers Paradise
Level 1, 'Piazza on the Boulevard', 3221 Gold Coast Highway,
Surfers Paradise
Tel: (07) 5539 0066
Fax: (07) 5539 0100
Email: *surfersparadise@harcourts.com.au*
Website: *www.harcourts.com.au*

L.J. Hooker Ashmore
Shop 4, Ashmore City Shopping Centre, Nerang Road
Tel: (07) 5510 1000
Fax: (07) 5510 1020
Email: *ashmore@ljh.com.au*
Website: *www.ljhooker.com.au/ashmore*

Hostels
Surfer's Paradise
Aquarius 44 Queen Street, Southport – (07) 5527 1300
Backpackers in Paradise 40 Peninsular Drive, Surfers Paradise –
    (07) 5538 4344 or 1800 268 621
British Arms International YHA Mariners Cove, 70 Seaworld Drive, Main
    Beach – (07) 5571 1776 or 1800 680 269 (toll free bookings)
Cheers Backpackers 8 Pine Avenue, Surfers Paradise – (07) 5531 6539
    or 1800 636 539
Couple O Days 18 Peninsular Drive, Surfers Paradise – (07) 5592 4200
Gold Coast International Backpackers Resort 28 Hamilton Avenue,
    Surfers Paradise – (07) 5592 5888
Islander Backpackers Resort – (07) 5538 8000

Sleeping Inn Surfers 26 Peninsular Drive Surfers Paradise –
    (07) 5592 4455
Surf n Sun Beachside Backpackers 3323 Gold Coast Highway,
    Surfers Paradise – (07) 5592 2363 or 1800 678 194
Surfers Paradise Backpackers Resort 2837 Gold Coast Highway,
    Surfers Paradise – (07) 5592 4677 or 1800 282 800
Trekkers 22 White Street Southport – (07) 5591 5616

TIP
► If you have a credit card, you can book your first few nights in some
hostels over the phone or internet. Go to: *www.hostelbrisbane.com.*

Work

Office work
MACQUARIE PEOPLE Level 6, 50 Cavill Avenue, Surfers Paradise –
    (07) 5526 2244
BROOK PERSONNEL Level 1, Evandale Place, 142 Bundall Road,
    Bundall – (07) 5510 3700
GROUP TRAINING AUSTRALIA GOLD COAST Level 1, Waterside East,
    Holden Place, Bundall – (07) 5556 7777
ACS – (07) 5510 8921
A P G GLOBAL Level 5, Waterside East Tower, Holden Place, Bundall –
    (07) 5557 5555
EVP (GOLD COAST) PTY LTD 3 Vespa Court, Bundall – (07) 5592 8880
GROUP TRAINING AUSTRALIA GOLD COAST – (07) 5574 2674
MACQUARIE PEOPLE Level 9, Corporate Centre, 1 Corporate Court,
    Bundall – (07) 5574 2005
MHS GROUP Level 2, 10 Holden Place, Bundall – (07) 5574 3411
MHS GROUP – MEDICAL Level 2, 10 Holden Place, Bundall –
    (07) 5574 3411

MY HR 3 Vespa Crs, Bundall – (07) 5592 8800

MY PEOPLE 3 Vespa Crs, Bundall – (07) 5592 8800

PINNACLE HOSPITALITY PEOPLE Level 2, Raptis Plaza, 4 The
Esplanade, Surfers Paradise – 1800 112 114

PRESIDENT SECURITY SERVICES (QLD) PTY LTD 48 The Promenade,
Isle Of Capri – (07) 5531 7766

QUEENSLAND APPRENTICESHIP SERVICES PTY LTD Level 1, F9,
47 Ashmore Rd, Bundall – (07) 5592 5232

Hospitality employers

The Gold Coast is packed with resorts, all with potential employers for
the working holiday maker.

Bars that may employ travellers on Working Holiday Makers (WHM) visas

The Rose & Crown Raptis Plaza, Cavill Mall – (07) 5531 5425

Avenue Restaurant & Saloon 4 Orchid Avenue – (07) 5592 1678

Billy's Beach House Hotel, Corner Hanlan Street and The Esplanade,
Surfers Paradise – (07) 5531 5666

The Bourbon Bar The Mark, Orchid Avenue – (07) 5538 0668

Fever Nightclub The Forum, 26 Orchid Avenue – (07) 5592 6222

Howl At The Moon Shop 7, Paradise Centre, Cavill Avenue –
(07) 5527 5522

Melbas 46 Cavill Avenue, Surfers Paradise – (07) 5538 7411

Santa Fe Gold 19 Orchid Avenue, Surfers Paradise – (07) 5592 2272

Shooters Saloon Bar The Mark, Shop 46, Orchid Avenue – (07) 5592 1144

The Sugar Shack Bar & Cafe 20 Orchid Avenue – (07) 5592 4850

The Drink Nightclub 4 Orchid Avenue – (07) 5570 6155

The Meeting Place Bar & Nightclub The Forum, 26 Orchid Avenue –
(07) 5526 2337

Tommy De's Corner Upton and Ashmore Roads, Bundall – (07) 5592 1599

Gold Coast hotels that may employ travellers on WHM visas

Concorde Hotel Gold Coast 42 Ferny Ave, Surfers Paradise – (07) 5539 0444

ANA Hotel Gold Coast 22 View Avenue, Surfers Paradise –
(07) 5579 1000
Australis Sovereign Hotel 138 Ferny Avenue, Surfers Paradise –
(07) 5579 3888
Gold Coast International Hotel Corner Gold Coast Highway and Staghorn
Avenue, Surfers Paradise – (07) 5584 1200
Islander Resort Hotel Surfers Paradise (07) 5538 8000
Surfers Paradise Marriott Resort, 158 Ferny Avenue, Surfers Paradise –
1800 809 090

Agencies
PINNACLE HOSPITALITY & TRAVEL PEOPLE Level 2, Raptis Plaza,
4 The Esplanade, Surfers Paradise, QLD 4217 – 1800 112 114

Nursing
Agencies in Brisbane
Check out these agencies in Brisbane for nursing jobs on the Gold
Coast:
CRITIQUE NURSES – (07) 3341 3999
HEALTHSTRA – 131148
OXLEY NURSING – (07) 3222 4800
QUEENSLAND NURSING AGENCY – (07) 3221 9883

Agencies on the Gold Coast
MHS GROUP – MEDICAL Level 2, 10 Holden Place, Bundall –
(07) 5574 3411

You will need to register as a nurse at:
Queensland Nursing Council, GPO Box 2928, Brisbane
Tel: (07) 3223 5110

Teaching
Agencies in Brisbane
DRAKE – (07) 3291 6099

Recognition of overseas qualifications

Firstly you should contact the department that deals with recognition of overseas qualifications, before you can register as a teacher in Queensland.

Skills Recognition Branch, Level 5, Education House, 30 Mary Street, Brisbane, Queensland 4000

Tel: (07) 3234 9900

www.trainandemploy.qld.gov.au

Registering as a teacher

In Queensland there are two different boards of teacher registration depending on whether you wish to work solely in government or public sector schools, or in both public and private schools. You will need to register as a teacher at:

www.education.qld.gov.au – Queensland Education Authority (for government schools)

... or *www.btr.qld.edu.au* – Board of Teacher Registration for all schools

Support

Internet cafes

Email Express, Shop 126, Ground Floor, Paradise Centre, Surfers Paradise

Global Gossip Gold Coast, 6 Beach Road, Surfers Paradise – (07) 5526 2280

Backpackers Information Centre

Transit Centre, Corner of Beach Road and Remembrance Drive, Surfers Paradise – (07) 5592 2911 or 1800 359 830

Open 8am-5.30pm daily

Gold Coast Tourism Bureau

Cavill Mall Surfers Paradise – (07) 5538 4419

Open Mon-Fri 8.30am-5.30pm, Sat 9am-5pm, Sun 9am-4pm

Coolangatta Tourist Information Centre
4 Wharf Street, Coolangatta – (07) 5536 4244 or 1800 674414
Open Mon-Sat 9am-5pm

Banks
ANZ – Surfers Paradise, 3171 Gold Coast Highway, QLD 4217
Westpac – Surfers Paradise, 3168 Gold Coast Highway, QLD 4217

Hospitals
Gold Coast Hospital, 108 Nerang Street – (07) 5571 8306

If you are a victim of crime or need community advice:
Police Headquarters
200 Roma Street, Brisbane, Queensland 4000
Tel: (07) 3364 6464
Tel: 000 Emergency

Cool places to hang out...
- Surfer's Paradise – the centre of the Gold Coast, jam packed with more clubs and bars than you can shake a stick at.
- The 70km of pristine beach. Oh yes...

Things to do at the Gold Coast...
- Did we mention the beach? Surfing and sunbathing are just two of the stressful activities on offer on the Gold Coast.
- If you get bored of the beach, then you can always head inland to the rainforest.

To avoid spending loads of money...
- Lie on the beach.
- Go for a trek in the sub-tropical Springbrook National Park and Lamington National Park.

Western Australia

A dramatic coastline, and a region full of mountains, gorges, stunning waterfalls, plus the Outback – and that's for those of you who get tired of Perth. Western Australia has got it all, and living and working here will give you the chance to indulge yourself in the great outdoors – from surfing to eating al fresco.

Perth

Why Perth?

Stunningly beautiful, clean beaches and fantastic weather – Perth represents much of what is best about Australia. It's a great place to visit – not least because it's a great place to get up close and personal with many of Australia's cutest (and oddest) animals. Make sure you get yourself up to Perth Zoo at some point during your stay to make friends with a kangaroo or feed a koala. The city is close to the Indian Ocean, and has a relaxed and cosmopolitan feel that will keep you on just the right side of chilled. Perth claims to be the sunniest city in Australia and its beaches are hard to beat. It makes an ideal starting point for exploring Western Australia in all its glory. You can swim with Dolphins at Monkey Mia, explore the National Parks at Yanchep and Nambung or swim on the reefs of Ningaloo.

AN INTERESTING PERTH FACT
► The Pavlova was invented in Perth.

Getting to and around Perth

Taxi: Taxi ranks are situated outside the Domestic and International terminals; you may have to pay your fare upfront, and the same fare stands whether it's just yourself or a group of you.

Bus: There is an Airport-City shuttle, operated by MYMA (tel: (08) 9475 2999), which runs between the airport's two terminals and the city; stops are located near hotels and hostels in Perth. The daily Fremantle Airport Shuttle service (tel: (08) 9335 1614) to Fremantle, a suburb of Perth, is also available.

Accommodation

Rentals
L.J. Hooker Rockingham
Suite 1, 9 Railway Terrace, Rockingham
Tel: (08) 9527 5055
Fax: (08) 9528 3988
Email: *rockingham@ljh.com.au*
Website: *www.ljhooker.com.au/rockingham*

Homestead Realty
478 Beaufort Street, Corner of Broome Street, Highgate
Tel: (08) 9227 6488
Website: *www.homestead-realty.com.au*

TOWN BY TOWN

USEFUL INFO
▶ To call Perth from the UK ring 0061 + 8 + eight digit number.

Hostels
Central
Beatty Lodge 235 Vincent Street – (08) 9227 1521
Britannia YHA 253 William Street – (08) 9328 6121
Downtowner Lodge 63 Hill Street – (08) 9325 6973
Exclusive Backpackers 158 Adelaide Terrace – (08) 9325 2852
Grand Central 379 Wellington Street – (08) 9421 1123
Murray St Hostel 119 Murray Street – (08) 9325 7627

Fremantle
Backpackers Home 49 Amherst Street – (08) 9336 6773
Backpackers Inn Freo 11 Pakenham Street – (08) 9431 7065
Cheviot Marina Backpackers 4 Beach Street – (08) 9433 2055
Old Firestation 18 Phillimore Street – (08) 9430 5454

Northbridge
12:01 East 195 Hay Street, Perth – (08) 9221 1666
Backpackers International Hostel Corner of Aberdeen and Lake Street –
    (08) 9227 9977
City Backpackers 156-158 Aberdeen Street – (08) 9328 6667
Coolibah Lodge 194 Brisbane Street – (08) 9328 9958
Indigo Backpackers 74 Aberdeen Street – (08) 9228 0648
Lonestar City Backpackers 17-21 Palmerston Street – (08) 9328 6667
Ozi Inn 282 Newcastle Street – (08) 9328 1222
Underground Backpackers 268 Newcastle Street – (08) 9228 3755

Work

Harvest work in Western Australia
On the next page are a few places where it's possible to get a job fruit
picking in Western Australia, along with all the best times to go and
how far away they are from the major cities. For a more expansive list,

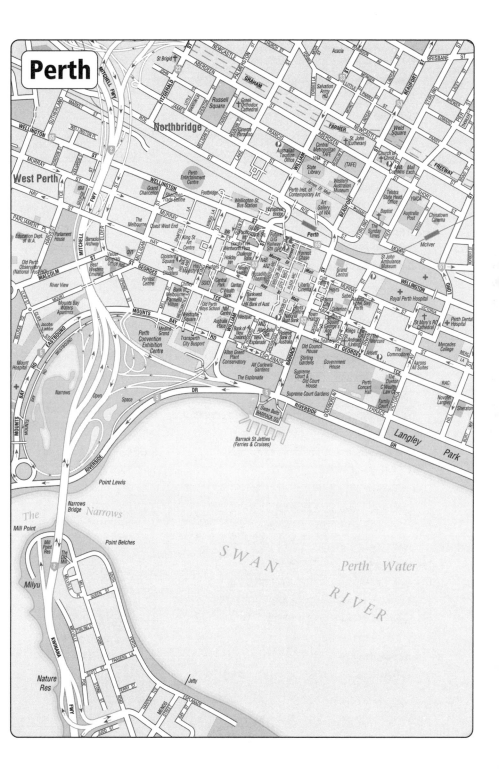

visit *www.jobsearch.gov.au/harvesttrail/* where jobs are listed and frequently updated or get information galore on each town.

Albany

Albany is a regional city in the Great Southern of Western Australia, 409km south of Perth, and is the oldest town in Western Australia.

February to April – *salmon fishing and processing*
March and April – *grape picking*
May and June – *olive picking*
June to September – *grape pruning*
July and August – *olive pruning*
October to May– *strawberries*

Kununurra

Kununurra is 3,228km north of Perth and 780km southwest of Darwin.

January to May – *citrus fruits*
April to September – *bananas*
May to October – *melons*
October to January – *mangoes*
Year round – *various other fruits and vegetables*

Office work

ADECCO – (08) 9461 4800
CATALYST – 133301
CHOICE – (08) 9321 2088
CHOICEONE – 1300 655 060
HAYS CALL CENTRE – (08) 9322 5383
JULIA ROSS – (08) 9486 9600
OFFICE ANGELS – (08) 9421 1522
RECRUITMENT SOLUTIONS – (08) 9481 2306
WESTAFF – (08) 9321 4104

Accountancy

ACCOUNTANCY PEOPLE – (08) 9486 1055

HAYS – (08) 9322 519
RECRUITMENT SOLUTIONS – (08) 9481 2306
FORRESTER MANNS – (08) 9324 2288

IT
COMPUTING VACANCIES – (08) 9221 3300
E HIRE – (08) 8211 9600
EXECOM – (08) 9429 6040
GLOBAL STAFFING – (08) 9382 3571
RECRUITMENT SOLUTIONS – (08) 9481 2306
TALENT INTERNATIONAl – (08) 9221 3300

Hospitality employers
Bars that may employ travellers on working holiday visas
Aberdeen Hotel 84 Aberdeen Street, Northbridge – (08) 9227 9361
Bog Fremantle 189 High Street, Fremantle (employs Irish travellers) –
    (08) 9336 7751
Bridie O'Reilly's 328 Barker Road, Subiaco – (08) 9381 8400
Elephant & Wheelbarrow 53 Lake Street, Northbridge – (08) 9228 4433
Louisiana's Restaurant Melbourne Hotel, Hay Street – (08) 9320 3333
The Lookout The Esplanade, Scarborough – (08) 9340 5738

Hotels that may employ travellers on WHVs
Burswood International Resort Casino – (08) 9362 7524
Greenwood Hotel 349 Warwick Road, Greenwood – (08) 9246 9711
Grosvenor Hotel 339 Hay Street – (08) 9325 3799
Inglewood Hotel Corner of Beaufort and Fifth Avenue, Mt Lawley –
    (08) 9370 5511
Sun Moon Resort Scarborough – (08) 9245 8000

Agencies
DUNHILL – (08) 9321 7712
McCOLL HOSPITALITY STAFF – (08) 9380 4711

Nursing

Agencies

AAA NURSES – (08) 9325 8100

CHOICEONE MEDITEMP – 1300 655 060

MEDITEMP – (08) 9321 2099

NT MEDIC – (08) 8941 1819

OXLEY – 1300 360 456

PERTH NURSING AGENCY – (08) 9370 3883

WESTERN AUSTRALIA NURSING AGENCY – 0800 9382 2288

You will need to register as a nurse at:

Nurses Board of Western Australia, PO Box 336, Nedlands, WA 6009
Tel: (08) 9386 8656

Teaching

Agencies

CHOICE PERSONNEL – (08) 9321 2011

EDCONNECT – (08) 9246 9007

WESTERN AUSTRALIA DEPARTMENT OF EDUCATION – (08) 9264 4111

You will need to register as a teacher at:

www.eddept.wa.edu.au – Department of Education and Training,
Western Australia.

For non-government schools contact individual employers about
teaching vacancies.

For more information contact:

Western Australia Overseas Qualifications Unit
7th Floor, 190 St Georges Terrace, Perth, WA 6000 –
Tel: (08) 9320 3747

Support

Internet cafes
Travellers Club 499 Wellington Street
Indigo Net Café & Lodge 256 West Coast Highway, Scarborough –
(08) 9245 3388
Global Grapevine 68 Aberdeen Street, Northbridge – (08) 9228 4330
Net Chat 196a William Street, Northbridge – (08) 9228 2011

Perth Visitors Centre
Corner of Wellington Street and Forrest Place – 1300 361 351

Student Uni Travel
513 Wellington Street – (08) 9321 8330

Banks
ANZ – 77 St Georges Terrace – (08) 9323 8111
Commonwealth – 150 St Georges Terrace – (08) 9482 6000
Westpac – 40 St Georges Terrace – 132032

Hospitals
Royal Perth Hospital, Wellington Street – (08) 9224 2244

If you are a victim of crime or need community advice:
Police Headquarters
Ground Floor, Curtin House, 60 Beaufort Street –
Tel: (08) 9223 3716
Tel: 131444 to contact nearest police station
Tel: 000 Emergency

Cool places to hang out...
The Deen 84 Aberdeen Street, Northbridge – (08) 9227 9361
Bog Perth 361 Newcastle Street – (08) 9228 3773
Church 69 Lake Street, Northbridge – (08) 9328 1065

Hip-E Club Corner of Oxford and Newcastle Street, Leederville – (08) 9227 8899

Left Bank Café Bar 15 Riverside Road, East Fremantle – (08) 9319 1315

The Post Office 133 Aberdeen Street, Northbridge – (08) 9228 0077

Things to do in Perth...

- Scarborough beach is only 15 minutes from the city and is very popular, both for its sands and the nightlife.
- Spend time in Kings Park, where you can enjoy the views of the city whilst having a picnic.
- Just south of Perth is Adventure World, a big amusement park with water attractions and bungee jumping.
- Take a trip to nearby Fremantle and explore the historic seaport.
- Check out the bars, clubs and cafes of Northbridge.
- Take the ferry to Rottnest Island from Perth and spend a day cycling round the island (no cars are allowed on the island) in search of the best beaches, diving and pubs.

TIPS

► If you do want to explore further from the city you will need a car. The desert to the east and Nambung National Park are not easily reachable by public transport.

Bunbury

Why Bunbury?

Bunbury is a great place to stay for a while. One of its main attractions are the dolphins on Koombana Beach, and it's also a great base if you want to visit Wellington National Park.

SOME BUNBURY FACTS
- The Bunbury Tower is known as the 'Milk Carton' because it is blue and white and looks a bit like ... a milk carton.
- It only became a city in 1979.

Accommodation

Rentals
Summit Realty
17 Molloy Street, Corner of Wittenoom and Symmons Street, Bunbury, WA 6230
Tel: (08) 9791 5555
Website: *www.Summitbunbury.com.au*

Lighthouse Realty South West
51 Marlston Drive, Bunbury WA 6230
Tel: (08) 9792 4000
Email: *sales@lighthouserealty.com.au*

Hostels

Dolphin Retreat Bunbury YHA 14 Wellington Street – (08) 9792 4690
Wander Inn 16 Clifton Street – (08) 9721 3242

TIP

► If you have a credit card, you can book your first few nights in some hostels over the phone or internet. Go to: *www.hostelperth.com*.

Work

Office work

JOBS SOUTHWEST 11 Bourke Street – (08) 9721 5033
FORREST PERSONNEL INCORPORATED 4 Plaza Street – (08) 9791 1672
THE APPRENTICE & TRAINEESHIP COMPANY – (08) 9725 6565
COMMUNITY DEVELOPMENT EMPLOYMENT PROGRAMME
    49 Spencer Street – (08) 9791 2466
FLEXI STAFF PTY LTD 34 Wittenoom St – (08) 9791 5032
GROUP TRAINING SOUTH WEST (INC) (Employment Services)
    123 Spencer Street – (08) 9791 3605
INTEGRATED GROUP Corner of Stephen and Victoria Streets –
    (08) 9791 4466
JOBFIND – (08) 9792 6100
JOBFIND CENTRE SHOP 23 Centrepoint Shopping Centre, Stirling
    Street, Bunbury WA 6230 – (08) 9792 9600
JOBFIND CENTRE Suite 1, 62 Wittenoom Street – (08) 9792 6100
JOBFUTURES 32 Wellington Street – (08) 9791 9022
JOBS SOUTH WEST 11 Bourke Street – (08) 9721 5033
MANPOWER Unit 1 50 Spencer Street – (08) 9792 9555
NEEDAC 100 Spencer Street – (08) 9791 1822
PVS WORKFIND 23 Wellington Street – (08) 9792 4755

READY WORKFORCE 20 Clifton Street – (08) 9792 4077

SKILLED Unit 2, 64 Spencer Street – (08) 9791 4878

SOUTH WEST PERSONNEL 31 Spencer Street – (08) 9721 8155

THE RECRUITMENT & EMPLOYMENT COMPANY 123 Spencer Street –
(08) 9791 4422

Hospitality employers
Bars that may employ travellers on Working Holiday Makers (WHM) visas

Prince Of Wales Bunbury – (08) 9721 2016

Burlington Hotel Bunbury – (08) 9721 2075

Hungry Hollow Tavern & Brasserie Bunbury – (08) 9791 5577

Parade Hotel Bunbury – (08) 9721 2933

Reef Hotel Bunbury – (08) 9791 6677

Rose Hotel Bunbury – (08) 9721 4533

Trafalgar's Hotel Bunbury – (08) 9721 2600

Bunbury hotels that may employ travellers on WHMs

Burlington Hotel 51 Victoria Street – (08) 9721 2075

Lighthouse Beach Resort – 1800 216 226

Lord Forrest Hotel Symmons Street – 1800 097 811

Parade Hotel 100 Stirling – (08) 9721 2933

Prince Of Wales Hotel 41 Stephen Street – (08) 9721 2016

Quality Hotel Lord Forrest Symmons Street – 1800 097 811

Quest Bunbury – (08) 9722 0777

Reef Hotel 12 Victoria Street – (08) 9791 6677

Rose Hotel Victoria Street – (08) 9721 4533

The Lighthouse Beach Resort Ocean Drive, Bunbury – (08) 9721 1311

The Sanctuary Golf Resort PO Box 1150 – (08) 9725 2777

Trafalgars Hotel 36 Victoria Street – (08) 9721 2600

Nursing
Agencies
PERTH NURSING AGENCY Suites 3 and 4, 771 Beaufort Street,
Mt Lawley, WA 6050
Tel: (08) 9370 3883

You will need to register as a nurse at:
Nurses Board of Western Australia, PO Box 336, Nedlands, WA 6009
Tel: (08) 9386 8656

Teaching
Agencies
CHOICE PERSONNEL – (08) 9321 2011
EDCONNECT – (08) 9246 9007
WESTERN AUSTRALIA DEPARTMENT OF EDUCATION – (08) 9264 4111

You will need to register as a teacher at:
www.eddept.wa.edu.au – Department of Education and Training,
Western Australia

For non-government schools contact individual employers about
teaching vacancies.

For more information contact:
Western Australia Overseas Qualifications Unit
7th Floor, 190 St Georges Terrace, Perth, WA 6000
Tel: (08) 9320 3747

Support

Internet cafes
The Internet Planet 79 Victoria Street – (08) 9791 6211

TOWN BY TOWN

Internet Outpost Broome at Eco Beach Backpackers, 16 Canarvon Street – (08) 8952 8730

Banks
ANZ – 118 Victoria Street, Bunbury
Westpac – 143 Victoria Street, Bunbury

Hospitals
Bunbury Regional Hospital, Corner of Bussell Highway and Robertson Drive – (08) 9722 1000

If you are a victim of crime or need community advice:
Bunbury Police Station
Wittenoom Street, Bunbury 6230
Tel: (08) 9722 2111
Tel: 131444 for non emergency
Tel: 000 Emergency

Cool places to hang out...
- Get up close and personal with the dolphins at Koombana Beach.
- Head to the CBD area for a few drinks and eat yourself silly at one of the area's great restaurants.

Things to do in Bunbury...
- Head to the Big Swamp – and meet the local kangaroos.
- Paddle with the dolphins at the Dolphin Discovery Centre.

Bunbury Visitor Information Centre:
Corner of Carmody Place and Haley Street, Bunbury
Tel: (08) 9721 7922
Open Mon-Sat 9am-5pm; Sun 9.30am-4.30pm

South Australia

Get ready for stunning beaches... and lots of wine! South Australia is the country's leading wine producing region, and with plenty of seasonal work, great weather and stunning scenery, it's a fantastic place to work and travel. Adelaide is also a great place to hang out for a while, with some of the best beaches in the country, as well as a vibrant nightlife.

Adelaide

Why Adelaide?

What a city! Perfectly planned to maximize the happiness of its citizens and its visitors, Adelaide is a fine example of how great life can be living in a modern city. It's got plenty of parks, a surplus of shops, masses of great markets and a roster of some of the world's most exotic foods served in a stunning array of great restaurants, all bundled up in a friendly and cosmopolitan package. Don't miss it!

AN INTERESTING ADELAIDE FACT
▶ There's apparently one pub built for every church in Adelaide. Sensible people.

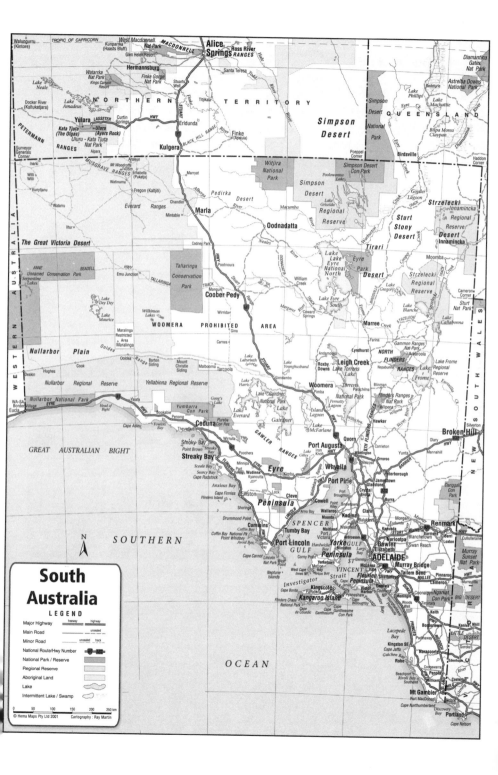

South Australia

LEGEND

Major Highway	freeway	highway
Main Road		unsealed
Minor Road	unsealed	track
National Route/Hwy Number		
National Park / Reserve		
Regional Reserve		
Aboriginal Land		
Lake		
Intermittent Lake / Swamp		

0   50   100   150   200   250 km

© Hema Maps Pty Ltd 2001   Cartography : Ray Martin

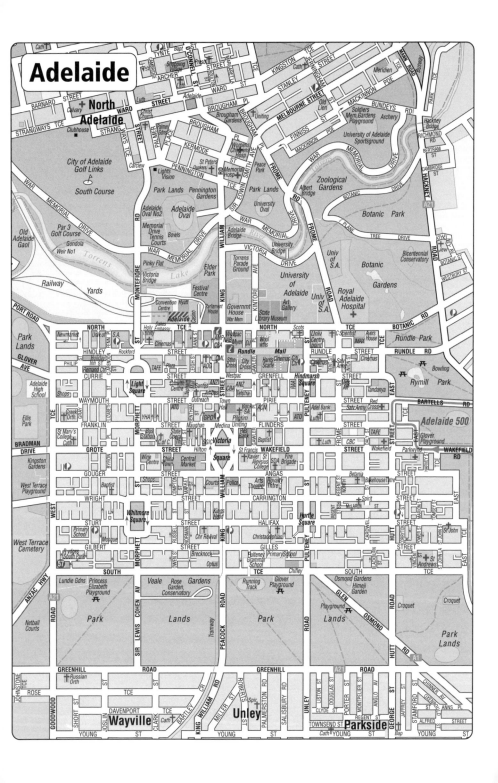

Getting to and around Adelaide

Taxi: There are taxi ranks at the Domestic and International terminal forecourts. It takes 15 minutes into the city centre. All the taxis are metered, so don't worry about being ripped off.

Bus: The Airport Bus operates every 30 minutes from the terminals providing a convenient link from the airport to the city centre.

Accommodation

Rentals
Phillis Real Estate Pty. Ltd.
97 Wright Street, Adelaide, South Australia 5000
Tel: (08) 8212 5899
Website: *www.phillisrealestate.com.au/*

L.J. Hooker Christies Beach
2/54 Beach Road
Tel: (08) 8326 2322
Fax: (08) 8326 2378
Email: *christiesbeach@ljh.com.au*
Website: *www.ljhooker.com.au/christiesbeach*

Hostels
Adelaide Backpackers Inn 112 Carrington Street – (08) 8223 6635
or 1800 247 725

TOWN BY TOWN

USEFUL INFO
▶ To call Adelaide from the UK ring 0061 + 8 + eight digit number.

155

Adelaide Backpackers Travel 139 Franklin Street – (08) 8231 2430
Adelaide Central Backpackers 110 Grote Street – (08) 8231 0639
Adelaide Central YHA 135 Waymouth Street – (08) 8223 6007
    or (08) 8414 3010
Adelaide City Backpackers 239 Franklin Street – (08) 8212 2668
Adelaide Travellers Inn/Backpackers Hostel 118 Carrington Street –
    (08) 8232 7022 or (08) 8224 0753
Blue Galah 1st floor 62 King William Street – 1800 555 322
Cannon Street Backpackers 11 Cannon Street – (08) 8410 1218
    or 1800 804 133
East Park Lodge 341 Angus Street – (08) 8223 1228
Glenelg Beach Resort 1-7 Moseley Street, Glenelg – (08) 8376 00(07)
    or 1800 066 422
Nomads Brecon Inn 11-13 Gilbert Street – (08) 8211 8985
    or 1800 990 009
Nomads Cumberland Arms Hotel 205 Waymouth Street –
    (08) 8231 3577
Rucksack Riders 257 Gilles Street – (08) 8232 0827
Sunny's Backpackers Hostel 139 Franklin Street – (08) 8231 2430
    or 1800 SUNNYS or 1800 BAKPAK
Tattersalls Adelaide City Backpackers 17 Hindley Street –
    (08) 8231 3225 or 1800 133 355

Work

Harvest work in South Australia

Below are a few places where it's possible to get a job fruit picking
in South Australia, along with all the best times to go and how far
away they are from the major cities. For a more expansive list, visit
www.jobsearch.gov.au/harvesttrail/ where jobs are listed and frequently
updated. You can also get information galore on each town.

► South Australia is famous for its wine, producing over 70% of the country's total, so there's plenty of temp work to be found here around harvest time.

The Barossa Valley does have its own employment agencies specifically for the grape harvest. Two of the most comprehensive are:

CREAM OF THE CROP
First Floor, 28 Greenhill Road, Wayville 5034
(08) 8274 2106
(08) 8274 2186
www.creamcareers.com.au
jobs@creamcareers.com.au

EXTRASTAFF PTY LTD
190 Fullarton Road, Dulwich SA 5065
(08) 8331 3688

Adelaide Hills

The Adelaide hills are located 20 minutes from the heart of Adelaide and boast great food, fine wines and stunning scenery.
February to April – *grape picking*
February to May – *apples and pears*
June to September – *grape pruning*
October to January – *cherry picking*
September to December – *vine training*

Waikerie

Waikerie is 170km north east of Adelaide and is one of the five major towns in South Australia's Riverland.
February to March – *grapes*
May to August – *grape vine pruning*

October to March – *stone fruit*
May to February – *citrus fruits*

Office work

JULIA ROSS – (08) 8212 9522

CATALYST RECRUITMENT – (08) 8293 2722

IPA PERSONNEL – (08) 8210 0600

SKILLED – 1300 366 606

QUALITY STAFF PTY LTD – (08) 8367 0366

OXLEY NURSING SERVICE PTY LTD – 1300 360 456

FORSTAFF (S.A.) – (08) 8359 7666

RECRUITMENT SOLUTIONS – (08) 8212 9111

ARA JOBS – (08) 8268 4444

ACTIVE SELECTION – (08) 8410 6800

TEMP-TEAM (Employment Services) – (08) 8410 6800

ADECCO – (08) 8409 9300

THE STAFF CONNECTION – (08) 8352 2732

TMP/HUDSON GLOBAL RESOURCES – (08) 8212 2677

AUSTRALIAN JOBSEARCH -136268

Accountancy

RECRUITMENT SOLUTIONS – (08) 8212 9111

HUDSON GLOBAL RESOURCES – (08) 8223 8800

HAYS ADELAIDE – (08) 8212 5242

IT

ADECCO – (08) 8409 9300

HANCOCK RECRUITMENT – 0500 550 090

AFFINITY – (08) 8304 1740

Hospitality employers
Bars that may employ travellers on Working Holiday Makers (WHM) visas
Hampshire Hotel – (08) 8231 5169

Arab Stead Hotel – (08) 8223 1015
Kent Town Hotel – (08) 8362 2116
The Stag – (08) 8223 2934
Royal Oak Hotel – (08) 8267 2488
The Earl of Aberdeen – (08) 8223 6433
The Planet – (08) 8359 2797

Adelaide hotels that may employ travellers on WHM visas
Adelaide City Fringe Apartments – 1800 180 128
Hotel Adelaide International – (08) 8267 3444
Taverner Hotel Group – (08) 8234 8833
Hotel Richmond – (08) 8223 4044
Medina Serviced Apartments – 1300 300 232
Pacific International Hotels – 1800 224 584
Worldsend Hotel – (08) 8231 9137
The Majestic Roof Garden Hotel – (08) 8223 0501

Agencies
ADELAIDE HOSPITALITY STAFFING – (08) 8359 2266
ADECCO – (08) 8409 9300
DUNHILL MANAGEMENT SERVICES – (08) 8271 5005

Nursing
Agencies
NURSING CARE SERVICES – (08) 8367 0044
ADECCO – (08) 8409 9300
DRAKE – (08) 8213 4141

You will need to register as a nurse at:
Nurses Board of South Australia
(postal) PO Box 7176, Hutt Street, Adelaide SA 5001
(location) 200 East Terrace, Adelaide SA 5000
Tel: (08) 8223 9700
registrations@nursesboard.sa.gov.au

Teaching

Agencies

ADECCO – (08) 8409 9300

TEMPORARY TEACHERS AGENCY OF SA – (08) 8272 8896

PROTOCOL TEACHERS ADELAIDE – 1800 246 436

For information on registering as a teacher :

Contact the Department of Education and Children's Services at *www.decs.sa.gov.au* .

Support

Internet cafes

Cafe.on.Net above Buongiornos Cafe, 187 Rundle Street –
    (08) 8359 2662
Cybersafety Cafe 69 Hindmarsh Square, Adelaide – (08) 8232 1577
Ngapartji Multimedia Centre 211 Rundle Street – (08) 8232 0839

South Australian Information Centre

18 King William Street, Adelaide – (08) 8303 2201 or 1300 655 276
Open Mon-Fri 8.30am-5pm; Sat-Sun 9am-2pm

Adelaide Travellers Contact Point

110 Franklin Street, Adelaide 5000

Banks

ANZ – 107 Gouger Street
Westpac – Adelaide, 2 Grenfell Street

Hospitals

Adelaide Clinic, 33 Park Terrace, Gilberton – (08) 8269 7307

If you are a victim of crime or need community advice:
Police Headquarters
30 Flinders Street, Adelaide 5000
Tel: (08) 8207 5000
Fax: (08) 8207 4525
Tel: 131444 to contact nearest police station
Tel: 000 Emergency

Cool places to hang out...
- The popular Glenelg beach.
- The Festival Centre – who needs the Sydney Opera House.
- The Barossa Valley – it's got over 50 wineries... oh yes!

Things to do in Adelaide...
- Soak up the sun on one of the city's great beaches.
- Enjoy the city parks which ring the city centre.
- Take a trip out to the unique and beautiful Kangaroo island, discovered by Captain Matthew Flinders and his cat Trim. We're not kidding...
- Force yourself to visit Haigh's Chocolate Factory, Australia's oldest chocolate maker. Oh, go on then, twist my arm...
- Try and be in town to catch the Adelaide Fringe – Australia's biggest arts festival and the second biggest in the world.

TIP
▶ If you're looking for a cultural break from the city's great bars and clubs, take a stroll down North Terrace where you'll find the Art Gallery of South Australia, the South Australian Museum and the Botanic Gardens.

Barossa Valley

Why the Barossa Valley?
The Barossa Valley is South Australia's largest wine region. It's a great place to head for seasonal and harvest work, if you get tired of the city and need to earn a bit of cash.

Accommodation

Rentals
Ray White Real Estate
97 Murray Street, Tanunda, SA 5352
Tel: (08) 8563 3866
Fax: (08) 8563 3193
E-mail: *Barossa.sa@raywhite.com*
Website: *www.raywhite.com*

Barossa Real Estate Pty. Ltd.
61 Murray Street, Tanunda, SA 5352
Tel: (08) 8563 3511
Fax: (08) 8563 0105
Website: *bvrealty@ozemail.com.au*

TIP
► Tanunda is the most central and convenient base if you're looking to do harvest work in the Barossa.

SOME BAROSSA VALLEY FACTS
► It has 45 wineries that produce around a quarter of Australia's wine.
► It's only 30km long by 14km wide.

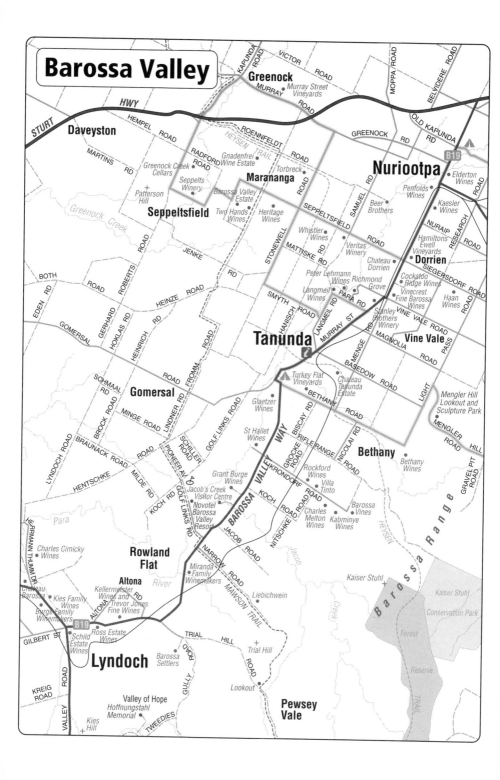

Hostels
Tanunda
Barossa Bunkhaus Corner of Barossa Valley Way and Nuraip Road, Nurioopta – (08) 8562 2260

Barossa Weintal Resort Murray Street – (08) 8563 2303

Novotel Barossa Valley Resort Golf Links Road, Rowland Flat – (08) 8524 0000

Tanunda Hotel 51 Murray Street – (08) 8563 2030

Valley Hotel Motel 73 Murray Street – (08) 8563 2039

Camping in the Barossa Valley
Tanunda Caravan & Tourist Park Barossa Valley Way, Tanunda, SA 5352 – (08) 8563 2784

Victor Harbor Holiday and Cabin Park Bay Road, Victor Harbor, SA 5211 – (08) 8552 1949

Berri Riverside Caravan Park Riverview Drive, Berri, SA 5343 – 1800 332 255

Aldinga Holiday Park Cox Road, Aldinga, SA 5173 – (08) 8556 3444

Barossa Caravan Park Barossa Valley Way, Lyndoch, SA 5351 – (08) 8524 4262

Rivers Edge Caravan Park 216 Princes Highway, Tailem Bend, SA 5260 – (08) 8572 3307

Westbrook Park River Resort Caravan & Tourist Park Princes Highway, Tailem Bend, SA 5260 – (08) 8572 3794

Work

Hospitality employers
Bars that may employ travellers on Working Holiday Makers (WHM) visas
Cafe Lanzerac and Wine Bar 109 Murray Street – (08) 8563 0322

Barossa Valley hotels that may employ travellers on WHM visas

Barossa Bunkhaus Corner of Barossa Valley Way and Nuraip Road, Nurioopta – (08) 8562 2260

Barossa Weintal Resort Murray St – (08) 8563 2303

Novotel Barossa Valley Resort Golf Links Road, Rowland Flat – (08) 8524 0000

Tanunda Hotel 51 Murray Street – (08) 8563 2030

Valley Hotel Motel 73 Murray Street – (08) 8563 2039

Agencies

CREAM OF THE CROP First Floor, 28 Greenhill Road, Wayville
Tel: (08) 82742106
www.creamcareers.com.au
jobs@creamcareers.com.au

EXTRASTAFF PTY LTD 190 Fullarton Road, Dulwich – (08) 83313688
www.rowanrecruitment.com.au
extrastaff.sa@rowanrecruitment.com.au

Support

Internet cafes

Tanunda Caravan and Tourist Park has an internet cafe on site –
Tel: (08) 8563 2784

Barossa Visitor Information Centre:

66 Murray Street Tanunda
Tel: 1800 812 662
www.barossa-region.org
Open Mon-Fri 9am-5pm; Sat-Sun 10am-4pm

Banks

ANZ – 44 Murray Street, Tanunda
Westpac – 59 Murray Street, Tanunda

If you are a victim of crime or need community advice:

Barossa Yorke Local Service Area

61 Murray Street, Nuriootpa

Tel: (08) 8560 9025

Tel: 131444 for non emergency

Tel: 000 Emergency

Cool places to hang out...

- If you want work, then head for the vineyards in February through to April.

Things to do in the Barossa Valley...

Apart from drinking wine, there are also plenty of things you can do in the Barossa that will earn you a bit of cash.

- Vine training: September – December.
- Grape pruning: June – September.
- Grape picking: January – April.

Northern Territory

If you like your landscapes big, red and dusty, then Australia's Northern Territory is one of the most beautiful expanses in the world. It is also home to much of Australia's rich Aboriginal culture, and many of its most iconic natural sights. Its 'Top End' is home to Darwin, a diverse and lively city that is well worth a visit. Head down south and you'll find Alice Springs and Uluru, known to us as Ayer's Rock.

....

Darwin

Why Darwin?

From being the home of an annual beer can boat race to being the gateway to some of Oz's most famous sights, Darwin has always been a pretty mixed up place. It's a fantastically ethnically diverse city, and this is reflected in the huge number of different foods you can eat and in the variety of music you can enjoy. But it is also a great base if you want to head out and see sights like Uluru (or Ayer's Rock), or the fabulous Kakadu National Park.

SOME DARWIN FACTS...

► There are over 170 different kinds of Bush food you can find in the Outback of the Northern Territory.

► Since 1964, crocodiles have been protected in the Northern Territory. Don't mess.

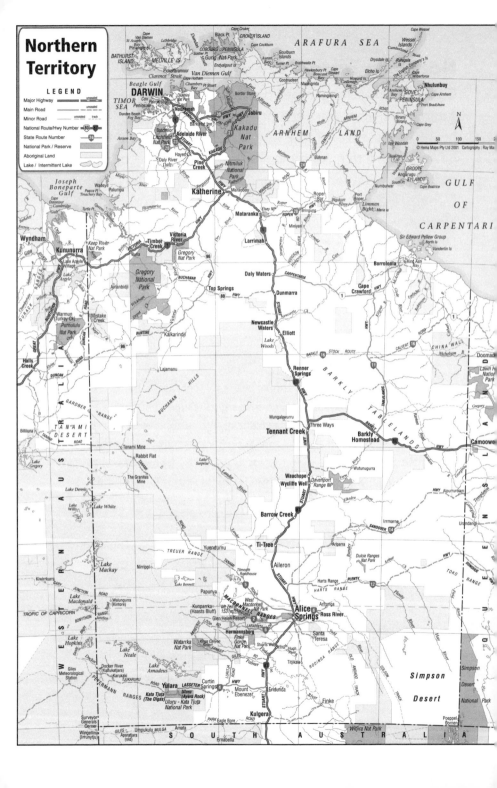

Northern Territory

LEGEND

Major Highway	sealed / unsealed
Main Road	sealed / unsealed
Minor Road	unsealed / track
National Route/Hwy Number	80 / 1
State Route Number	24
National Park / Reserve	
Aboriginal Land	
Lake / Intermittent Lake	

© Hema Maps Pty Ltd 2001 Cartography: Ray Ma...

0   50   100   150

ARAFURA SEA

GULF OF CARPENTARIA

ARNHEM LAND

DARWIN

TIMOR SEA

Beagle Gulf

Joseph Boneparte Gulf

WESTERN AUSTRALIA

QUEENSLAND

SOUTH AUSTRALIA

Simpson Desert

TANAMI DESERT

TROPIC OF CAPRICORN

Alice Springs

Tennant Creek

Katherine

Kakadu Nat Park

Gregory National Park

BARKLY TABLELANDS

Getting to and around Darwin

Bus: Darwin Airport Shuttle (1800 358 945 for use within Northern Territory or (08) 8981 5066 for use in other States) operates daily between Darwin International Airport and Darwin City Centre. Group prices are available and they are willing to take you to other locations as long as you book first.

Taxi: A large taxi rank is located at the front of the Terminal.

Accommodation

Rentals
L.J. Hooker Darwin
110 Mitchell Street
Tel: (08) 8924 0900
Fax: (08) 8981 9197
Email: *darwin@ljh.com.au*
Website: *www.ljhooker.com.au/darwin*

Hostels
YHA Northern Territory – (08) 8981 2560
Alice Lodge Backpackers – (08) 8953 1975
Annie's Place – (08) 8952 1545
Coco's House – (08) 8971 2889
Darwin City Lodge – (08) 8941 1295
Darwin's International YHA – (08) 8981 3995
Elke's Backpackers Resort & Budget Accommodation – (08) 8952 8422

TOWN BY TOWN

USEFUL INFO
▶ To call Darwin from the UK ring 0061 + 8 + eight digit number.

Golden Sands – (08) 8978 5075
Kookaburra Lodge – (08) 8971 0257
Leprechaun Motel & Caravan Park – (08) 8984 3400
Melaleuca Lodge – (08) 8956 1091
Banyan View Lodge – (08) 8981 8644
Chilli Backpackers – (08) 8941 9722 or 1800 351 313
Frogshollow Backpackers – (08) 8941 2600 or 1800 068 686
Gecko Lodge – (08) 8981 5569 or 1800 811 250
Globetrotters Lodge – (08) 8981 5385 or 1800 800 798

Work

Harvest work in Darwin

Below are a few places where it's possible to get a job fruit picking in the Northern Territory, along with all the best times to go and how far away they are from the major cities. For a more expansive list, visit *www.jobsearch.gov.au/harvesttrail/* where jobs are listed and frequently updated, and get information galore on each town.

Darwin

All year round – *bananas*
All year round – *vegetables (especially Asian vegetables)*
All year round – *cut flowers*
May to October – *melons*
September to April – *citrus fruits*
October and November – *mangoes*
November to February – *rambutans*

Katherine

All year round – *bananas*
All year round – *citrus fruits*
May to October – *melons*
October and November – *mangoes*

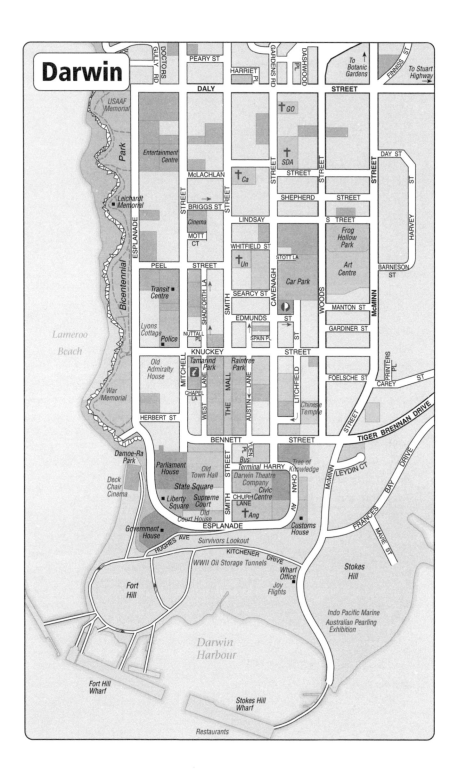

Darwin

PEARY ST
HARRIET ST
DALY **STREET**
GULLY RD
DOCTORS
GARDENS RD
DASHWOOD PL
FINNISS ST
To Botanic Gardens
To Stuart Highway

USAAF Memorial
Park
† GO
Entertainment Centre
STREET
† SDA
STREET
STREET
DAY ST
McLACHLAN
STREET
† Ca
Leichardt Memorial
ESPLANADE
STREET
SHEPHERD STREET
HARVEY ST
BRIGGS ST
Cinema
LINDSAY STREET
S TREET
MOTT CT
WHITFIELD ST
Frog Hollow Park
BARNESON ST
PEEL STREET
† Un
STOTT LA
Art Centre
CAVENAGH
Bicentennial
SHADFORTH LA
SEARCY ST
Car Park
McMINN
Transit Centre
SMITH
STREET
MANTON ST
Lameroo Beach
Lyons Cottage
■ Police
EDMUNDS
ST
WOODS
GARDINER ST
NUTTALL PL
SPAIN PL
KNUCKEY STREET
War Memorial
Old Admiralty House
MITCHELL
Tamarind Park
Raintree Park
FOELSCHE ST
PRINTERS PL
CHAPEL LA
WEST
THE MALL
AUSTIN LA
LITCHFIELD
Chinese Temple
CAREY ST
HERBERT ST
STREET
BENNETT STREET
TIGER BRENNAN DRIVE
Damoe-Ra Park
Parliament House
Old Town Hall
Bus Terminal
Tree of Knowledge
LEYDIN CT
Deck Chair Cinema
State Square
HARRY
Darwin Theatre Company
Civic Centre
CHAN AV
McMINN
■ Liberty Square
Supreme Court
CHURH LANE
FRANCES BAY DRIVE
Government House
Old Court House
ESPLANADE
† Ang
Customs House
MAVIE ST
Stokes Hill
HUGHES AVE
Survivors Lookout
KITCHENER DRIVE
WWII Oil Storage Tunnels
Wharf Office
Joy Flights
Indo Pacific Marine
Australian Pearling Exhibition
Fort Hill
Darwin Harbour
Fort Hill Wharf
Stokes Hill Wharf
Restaurants

Office work

SKILLED – 1300 366 606

OXLEY NURSING SERVICE PTY LTD – 1300 360 456

ADECCO – (08) 8936 2300

TMP/HUDSON GLOBAL RESOURCES – (08) 8941 5200

AUSTRALIAN JOBSEARCH – 136268

JULIA ROSS RECRUITMENT – 1300 139 922

JOB NETWORK – 131715

MANPOWER – 132502

A1 EMPLOYMENT SERVICE – (08) 8981 9355

ANGLICARE-EMPLOYABILITY – (08) 8972 1571

AVANT PERSONNEL – (08) 8941 2299

DRAKE – (08) 8924 3333

Accountancy

ADECCO DARWIN – (08) 8936 2300

DUNHILL MANAGEMENT SERVICES – (08) 8981 9944

IT

DRAKE PERSONNEL – (08) 8924 3333

ADECCO – (08) 8936 2300

Hospitality employers
Bars that may employ travellers on Working Holiday Makers (WHM) visas

Roma Bar 30 Cavenagh Street – (08) 8981 6729

Rorke's Drift Bar Cafe 46 Mitchell Street – (08) 8941 7171

Squires Tavern 3 Edmund Street – (08) 8981 9761

Mississippi Queen (08) 8981 3358

Kitty O'Shea's Irish Bar & Cafe – (08) 8941 7947

Blue Heeler Bar – (08) 8941 7945

Shenannigans Irish Pub – (08) 8981 2100

The Cavenagh – (08) 8941 6383

Victoria Hotel – (08) 8981 4011

Globe Trotters Bar & Lodge – (08) 8981 5385
Discovery Nightclub – (08) 8942 3300
Gilligans Piano Bar On The Wharf – (08) 8941 1909

Darwin hotels that may employ travellers on WHM visas

Value Inn Darwin 50 Mitchell Street, Darwin – (08) 8981 4733
Botanic Gardens Apartments 17 Geranium Street, Darwin –
    (08) 8946 0300
MGM Grand Darwin Gilruth Avenue, Mindil Beach, Darwin –
    (08) 8943 8888
Darwin Central Hotel 21 Knuckey Street, Darwin – (08) 8944 9000
Carlton Hotel Darwin The Esplanade, Darwin – (08) 8980 0800
The Cavenagh 12 Cavenagh Street, Darwin – (08) 8941 6383
Holiday Inn Darwin 122 The Esplanade, Darwin – (08) 8981 5388
Mirambeena Resort Darwin 64 Cavenagh Street, Darwin –
    1800 891 100

Agencies

ADECCO DARWIN – (08) 8936 2300
DUNHILL MANAGEMENT SERVICES – (08) 8981 9944

Nursing
Agencies

N.T. MEDIC PTY LTD – (08) 8941 1819
OXLEY NURSING SERVICE PTY LTD – 1300 360 456
ADECCO DARWIN – (08) 8936 2300
DRAKE PERSONNEL – (08) 8924 3333

You will need to register as a nurse at:

Nurses Board of the Northern Territories
(postal) PO Box 4221, Darwin NT 0801
(location) 10th Floor, NT House, 22 Mitchell Street, Darwin NT 0800
Tel: (08) 8999 4157
professionalboards.ths@nt.gov.au

Teaching

Agencies

ADECCO DARWIN
Tel: (08) 8936 2300
www.teachers.on.net

For information on registering as a teacher:
Teacher Registration Board
PO Box 1675, Darwin, NT 0801
Tel: (08) 8999 5963 or +61 8 8999 5963 (from outside Australia)
trb@nt.gov.au

Support

Internet cafes
SauS IT Internet Cafe Shop10, Paspalis Centrepoint Building, Smith
     Street Mall – (08) 8941 0622
Internet Outpost Darwin at Transit Centre, 69 Mitchell Street –
     (08) 8981 0720

Northern Territory Government Tourist Bureau
31 Smith Street, Darwin
Tel: (08) 8981 6611
www.nttc.com.au.

Darwin Student Uni Travel
50 Mitchell Street, Darwin
Tel: (08) 8981 3388

Darwin Travellers Contact Point
11 Knuckley Street, Darwin
Tel: (08) 8941 0070

Banks
ANZ – 69 Smith Street, Darwin, NT 0800
Westpac – The Mall, 24 Smith Street, Darwin, NT 0800

Hospital
Royal Darwin Hospital, Rocklands Drive
Tel: (08) 8922 8888

If you are a victim of crime or need community advice:
Police Headquarters
Northern Territory Police Fire and Emergency Services
Mitchell Centre, PO Box 39764, Winnellie NT 0821
Tel: (08) 8999 5511
Tel: 131444 to contact nearest police station
Tel: 000 Emergency

Cool places to hang out...
* Eat, drink and be merry at Mindil Beach Sunset Markets.
* Eat yourself silly at Lizards Bar & Outdoor Grill.

Things to do in Darwin...
* Hand feed the fish at Aquascene – get up close and personal with a mullet at 28 Doctors Gully Road.
* Eat! Darwin has got some great restaurants – largely down to its many different ethnic groups.
* Browse Mindil Beach Market – eat, shop, shop, eat!

Darwin Visitor Centre:
Corner of Mitchell and Knuckey Streets, Darwin
Tel: (08) 8936 2499
Open Mon-Fri 9am-5pm, Sat 9am-3pm; Sun 10am-3pm

Alice Springs

Why Alice Springs?
Alice Springs is a great place to stay because of its situation – it's the perfect base for exploring the MacDonnell Ranges, as well as Uluru, better known to us as Ayer's Rock.

Accommodation

Rentals
L.J. Hooker Alice Springs
Centrepoint, 12 Gregory Terrace
Tel: (08) 8952 6333
Fax: (08) 8953 0814
Email: *alicesprings@ljh.com.au*
Website: *www.ljhooker.com.au/alicesprings*

Hostels
Alice Lodge Backpackers 4 Mueller Street – (08) 8952 8855
Elke's Backpackers Resort 39 Gap Road – (08) 8952 8422
    or 1800 633 354
Annie's Place 4 Traeger Avenue – (08) 8952 1545
Toddy's Backpackers Resort 41 Gap Road – (08) 8952 1322
    or 1800 806 240
Melanka Backpackers 94 Todd Street – (08) 8952 4744 or
    1800 815 066
Ossie's Hostel Corner Lindsay Avenue/Warburton Street – 1800 628 211

SOME ALICE SPRINGS FACTS...
► It's about 1,000km away from the nearest comparably-sized town!
► It is also tiny – only 26,000 people live there.

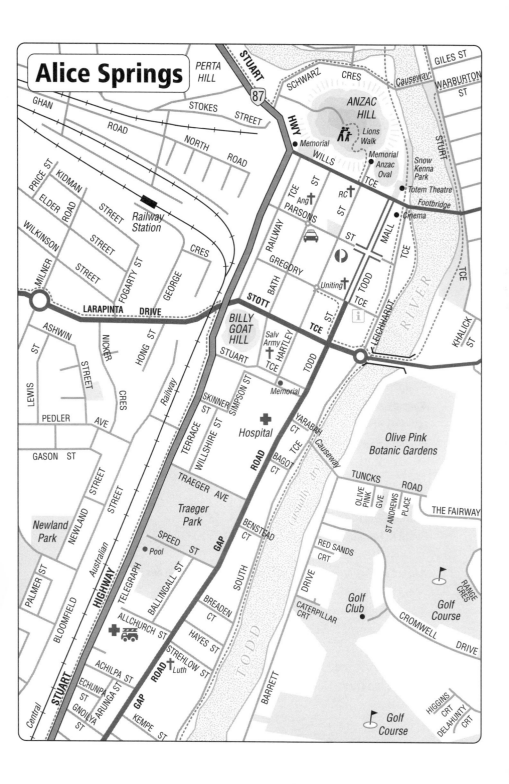

Pioneer YHA Hostel Corner Leichhardt and Parsons Streets –
(08) 9852 8855
Alice's Secret Travellers Inn 6 Khalick Street – (08) 8952 8686
or 1800 783 633

Work

Office work

WORKZONE Level 1, 8 Gregory Terrace – (08) 8952 4300
www.workzone.com.au, info@workzone.com.au
GROUP TRAINING NORTHERN TERRITORY (Employment Service)
Alice Plaza – (08) 8953 2622
ITEC EMPLOYMENT Cinema Complex Leichardt Terrace –
(08) 8952 2422
NEW APPRENTICESHIPS CENTRE Alice Plaza – 1300 137 130

Hospitality employers
Bars that may employ travellers on Working Holiday Makers
(WHM) visas
Bojangles Saloon & Restaurant 80 Todd Street – (08) 8952 2873
www.boslivesaloon.com.au
The Limerick Inn at Lasseters Hotel Casino, 93 Barrett Drive –
(08) 8950 7777
Melanka 94 Todd Street – (08) 8952 4744
Firkin & Hound 21 Hartley Street – (08) 8953 3033

Alice Springs hotels that may employ travellers on WHM visas
Larapinta Motel 3 Larapinta Drive – (08) 8952 7255
Alice Springs Plaza Hotel 94 Todd Street – (08) 8952 2233
Desert Rose Inn 15 Railway Terrace – (08) 8952 1411
Voyages Alice Springs Resort 34 Stott Terrace – (08) 8951 4545
Todd Tavern 1 Todd Mall – (08) 8952 1255 Hotels
Mercure Inn Oasis 10 Gap Road – (08) 8952 1444

Alice Springs Holidays – (08) 8953 1411
Lasseters Hotel Casino 93 Barrett Drive – (08) 8950 7777
Novotel Outback Alice Springs 46 Stephens Road, Alice Springs –
(08) 8952 6100

Agencies

WORKZONE Level 1 8 Gregory Tce – (08) 8952 4300
www.workzone.com.au, info@workzone.com.au
GROUP TRAINING NORTHERN TERRITORY (Employment Services)
Alice Plaza – (08) 8953 2622
ITEC EMPLOYMENT Cinema Complex, Leichardt Terrace – (08) 8952 2422
NEW APPRENTICESHIPS CENTRE Alice Plaza – 1300 137 130

Nursing
Agencies

For nursing positions in Alice Springs, check out what's available with
these agencies in Darwin.
N.T. MEDIC PTY LTD – (08) 8941 1819
OXLEY NURSING SERVICE PTY LTD – 1300 360 456
ADECCO DARWIN – (08) 8936 2300
DRAKE PERSONNEL – (08) 8924 3333

You will need to register as a nurse at:

Nurses Board of the Northern Territories
(postal) PO Box 4221, Darwin, NT 0801
(location) 10th Floor NT House, 22 Mitchell Street, Darwin, NT 0800
Tel: (08) 8999 4157
professionalboards.ths@nt.gov.au

Teaching

Agencies

Get in touch with agencies in Darwin if you're looking for teaching work in Alice Springs.

ADECCO DARWIN – (08) 8936 2300

www.teachers.on.net

For information on registering as a teacher:

Teacher Registration Board

PO Box 1675, Darwin, NT 0801

Tel: (08) 8999 5963 or +61 8 8999 5963 (from outside Australia)

trb@nt.gov.au

Support

Internet cafes

Internet Outpost at Melanka Backpackers, 94 Todd Street

Tel: (08) 8952 8730

Travellers Contact Point

Alice Springs

Shop 1, 72 Todd Street, Alice Springs, NT 0870

Tel: (08) 8953 5599

Tourist Information Centre

Gregory Terrace, Alice Springs

Tel: (08) 8952 5800

Open Mon-Fri 8.30am-5.30pm; Sat-Sun 9am-4pm

Banks

ANZ – Corner of Parson Street and Todd Street, Alice Springs, NT 0870

Westpac – 19 Todd Mall, Alice Springs, NT 0870

Hospitals
Alice Springs Hospital, Gap Road
Tel: (08) 8951 7777

If you are a victim of crime or need community advice:
Northern Territory Police, Fire and Emergency Services
Southern Region
PO Box 2630
Tel: (08) 8951 8888.

Cool places to hang out...
- Chill out at Bar Doppio and indulge yourself in some great veggie and vegan food.
- Get a flavour of the old Outback life at Bojangles Saloon & Restaurant.

Things to do in Alice Springs...
- Visit Uluru (Ayer's Rock) and the Olgas, and see some of Oz's most spectacular sights.
- Head out into the desert – it's big, it's dry and it's all around you in Alice Springs.

Australian Capital Territory (ACT)

Australia's capital is often passed over in favour of its more famous cities – ask people what the capital of Australia is and you can bet a lot of them will say Sydney! But Australia's capital has got a lot to offer – especially if you are looking to get office work while you're in Oz. As the nation's main administrative centre there are plenty of companies looking for temporary staff, so get your suit on and get job hunting!

Canberra

Why Canberra?

Australia's capital is often forgotten in favour of brasher and more well-known cities like Sydney, but there's plenty here to keep any visitor occupied, whether they want to stay for a weekend or a few months. Apart from the fact that there is plenty of work here, (as you'd expect from the nation's capital), the city also has plenty to seduce you. It is fantastically green, with plenty of parks and green spaces, and is a relaxing and refreshing place – perfect for when you get tired of the city's many great bars and clubs!

SOME CANBERRA FACTS...

► Canberra was designed by an American.
► And it was built in 1927.

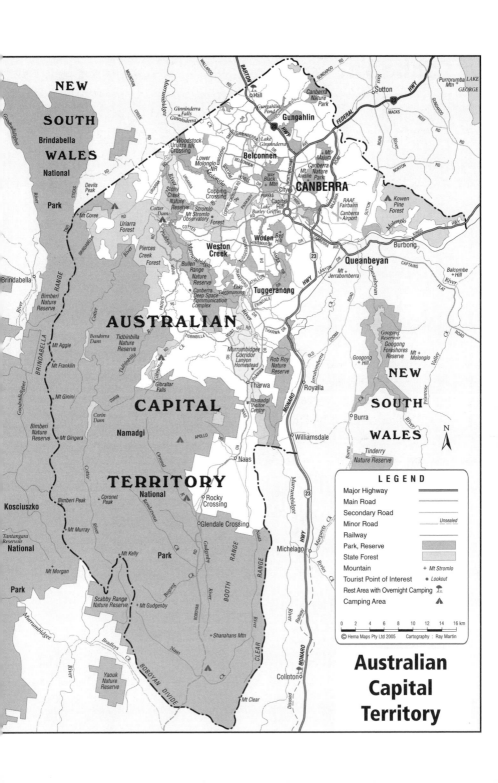

Australian Capital Territory

LEGEND

Major Highway	
Main Road	
Secondary Road	
Minor Road	*Unsealed*
Railway	
Park, Reserve	
State Forest	
Mountain	+ Mt Stromlo
Tourist Point of Interest	• Lookout
Rest Area with Overnight Camping	
Camping Area	▲

0 2 4 6 8 10 12 14 16 km

© Hema Maps Pty Ltd 2005   Cartography : Ray Martin

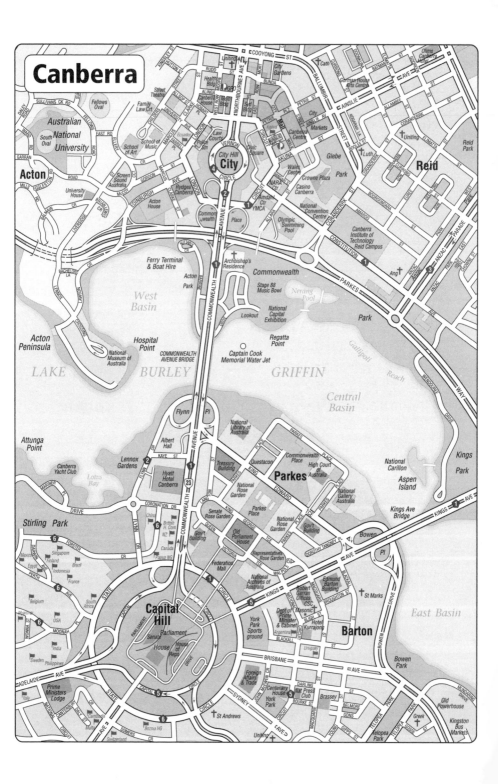

Getting to and around Canberra

Bus: The Airliner shuttle bus service operates Monday to Friday travelling to and from the Airport and Canberra city. You can pick up the Airliner bus from the central terminal right outside the main doors. The fare is only $7 one way and $12 return.

Taxi: Taxis are available at all times of the day from the front of the Terminal. An average fare to the city or Parliament House is $14 to $16

Accommodation

Rentals
L.J. Hooker Canberra City
1st Floor, 182–200 City Walk
Tel: (02) 6249 7700
Fax: (02) 6249 1477
Email: *canberracity@ljh.com.au*
Website: *www.ljhooker.com.au/canberracity*

Hostels
Canberra Backpackers 7 Akuna Street – (02) 6257 3999 or 1800 300 488
Canberra YHA Hostel 191 Dryandra Street, O'Connor – (02) 6248 9155
City Walk Hotel 2 Mort Street – (02) 6257 0124
Kingston Hotel 73 Canberra Avenue, Kingston – (02) 6295 0123
Victor Lodge 29 Dawes Street, Kingston – (02) 6295 7777

TIP
► If you have a credit card, you can book your first few nights in some hostels over the phone or internet. Go to: *www.hostelcanberra.com.*

Canberra Hotels – www.canberra.travelreporter.com
Kingston Hotel Backpackers 73 Canberra Avenue – (02) 6295 0123
Canberra City YHA 7 Akuna Street, Canberra City – (02) 6248 9155

Work

Harvest work in The Australian Capital Territory

The Australian Capital Territory is located right in the heart of New
South Wales, so for all your fruit picking needs, visit *www.jobsearch.gov.au/
harvesttrail/* which will be able to direct you to the nearest fruit picking
farms. A few places that should have work are:

Batlow

In the foothills of the Snowy mountains, Batlow is situated 443km
south west of Sydney.
March to May – *apples*
June to November – *pruning*
October to April – *stone fruits*

Griffith

Griffith proudly produces 20% of Australians wine and is a few
hundred kilometres to the north west of Canberra.
All year round – *vegetables*
All year round – *oranges*
All year round – *rice*
All year round – *stone fruits*

Office work

ALLIANCE RECRUITING Level 1, Bailey's Corner, 143 London Crescent –
    (02) 6262 7777
PEOPLE OPTIONS Bailey's Corner, London Crescent – (02) 6262 8999
OMEGA PERSONNEL PTY LTD AMP Building, Hobart Place –
    (02) 6248 5588

CATALYST RECRUITMENT SYSTEMS LIMITED Level 8, 1 Hobart Place –
133301
ELAN IT RECRUITMENT SOLUTIONS Level 4, AMP Building, 1 Hobart
Place – (02) 6200 3444
MANPOWER AMP Building, Level 4, 1 Hobart Place – (02) 6200 3399
THE GREEN & GREEN GROUP Level 9, AMP Tower, 1 Hobart Place –
(02) 6257 5600
ALLIANCE LEGAL Level 5, 161 London Crescent – (02) 0257 4544
KOWALSKI RECRUITMENT 175 London Crescent – (02) 6230 6636
CAREERNET INTERNATIONAL Level 6, 39 London Crescent –
(02) 6230 5339
LEE HECHT HARRISON Level 6, 39 London Crescent – (02) 6263 5999
LEGAL PERSONNEL Level 3, Canberra House, 40 Marcus Clarke Street –
(02) 6257 1010
PROFESSIONAL CAREERS AUSTRALIA PTY LTD Level 3, 40 Marcus
Clarke Street – (02) 6257 1010 or 1300 662 006
CAREERS UNLIMITED PTY LTD 17-21 University Avenue –
(02) 6257 8299
FINITE IT RECRUITMENT SOLUTIONS Level 1, CML Building,
17-21 University Avenue – (02) 6249 7877
IT & T CAREERS Level 1, CML Building, 17-21 University Avenue –
(02) 6249 7877
FRONTIER GROUP AUSTRALIA PTY LTD Level 1, 33 Ainslie Avenue –
(02) 6230 0355
ACCOUNTEMPS 12 Moore Street – (02) 6230 7587
SMALLS RECRUITING 12 Moore Street – (02) 6230 1011
DONINGTON (ACT) PTY LTD Level 12, 15 London Crescent –
(02) 6230 0798
SELECT APPOINTMENTS Level 12, 15 London Crescent –
(02) 6278 0088
CHANDLER MACLEOD GROUP Level 1, 10 Rudd Street – (02) 6230 4778
TELUS Level 1, 10 Rudd Street – (02) 6243 6133
KOWALSKI CONSULTING Level 1, Ethos House, 28-36 Ainslie Avenue –
(02) 6230 6636

Hospitality employers
Bars that may employ travellers on Working Holiday Makers (WHM) visas

Loui 111 Alinga Street – (02) 6230 0626

The Gods Cafe & Bar University Avenue – (02) 6248 5538

Yum Yum Tree 143 London Crescent – (02) 6247 9464

Cafe Moda Shop DF, 21 Canberra Centre – (02) 6257 1313

Chats Café Canberra School of Arts ANU – (02) 6249 5847

Club Asmara 128 Bunda Street – (02) 6257 6633

Blue Gum Café 71 Northbourne Avenue – (02) 6247 2414

Country Cravings 148 Bunda Street – (02) 6257 1595

Clares Café 38 Akuna Street – (02) 6247 6828

Courtyard Café Unit 3, 7 Geils Court – (02) 6285 3147

Bay Tree Café 40 Allara Street – (02) 6247 4751

Cafe Blue 81 Denison Street, Deakin – (02) 6282 8416

Tulip's Café 8 Beltana Road, Pialligo – (02) 6249 6118

Heaven Nite Club Bunda Street – (02) 6257 6180

The Phoenix 21 East Row, Civic – (02) 6247 1606

Civic Pub 8 Lonsdale Street, Braddon – (02) 6248 6488

Gypsy Bar 131 City Walk – (02) 6247 7300

King O'Malleys 131 City Walk – (02) 6257 0111

Filthy McFadden's 62 Jardine Street, Green Square, Kingston – (02) 6239 5303

Bobby McGee's 1 London Circuit – (02) 6257 7999

Club Mombasa 128 Bunda Street – 0419 609 106 (info line)

Insomnia 50 Northbourne Avenue – (02) 6248 0102

Canberra hotels that may employ travellers on WHM visas

Pavilion on Northbourne Hotel and Serviced Apartments 242 Northbourne Ave – (02) 6247 6888

The Phoenix 21 East Row – (02) 6247 1606

Novotel Canberra 65 Northbourne Avenue – (02) 6245 5000

Waldorf Apartment Hotel 2 Akuna Street – 1800 188 388

Aree Bar 7 Akuna Street – (02) 6257 3062

Canberra City Accommodation 7 Akuna Street – (02) 6257 3999
City Walk Hotel Corner of City Walk and Mort Street – (02) 6257 0124
Rydges Lakeside London Circuit – (02) 6247 6244

Agencies
ADECCO CANBERRA 1/115 Canberra Avenue – (02) 6284 6999
DUNHILL MANAGEMENT SERVICES – CANBERRA Level 9, 60 Marcus
    Clarke Street
HAYS CANBERRA Level 3, 54 Marcus Clarke Street

Nursing
Agencies
ADECCO CANBERRA 1/115 Canberra Avenue – (02) 6284 6999
DRAKE PERSONNEL CANBERRA Drake House, 35-37 London Circuit –
    (02) 6249 7366
HAYS CANBERRA Level 3, 54 Marcus Clarke Street – (02) 6257 6344
HEALTH SERVICES AUSTRALIA Level 1, 15 Bowes Street –
    (02) 6269 2001

TIP
▶ Some agencies recruit all kinds of medical staff, including
administrative people.

You will need to register as a nurse at:
Nurses Board of the ACT
PO Box 976, Civic Square ACT 2608
6th Floor, FAI House 197 London Circuit, Canberra City 2600
Tel: (02) 6205 1599
Fax: (02) 6205 1602

TOWN BY TOWN

Teaching

Agencies

ADECCO CANBERRA, 1/115 Canberra Avenue – (02) 6284 6999

Independent schools

Association of Independent Schools of the ACT Inc (AISACT)
12 Thesiger Court, Deakin, ACT 2600
Tel: (02) 9299 2845
aisact@ais.act.edu.au
www.ais.act.edu.au

Contact individual employers for vacancies in independent schools in ACT.

For information on registering as a teacher in Canberra

The Australian Capital Territory (ACT) Department of Education and Training – *www.decs.act.gov.au*

Support

Internet cafes

Cyberchino, 33 Kennedy Street – 06 295 7844

Canberra Tourism

330 Northbourne Avenue
www.canberratourism.com.au
Tel: (02) 6205 0044 or 1300 554 114
Open Mon-Fri 9am-5.30pm; Sat-Sun 9am-4pm

Banks

ANZ – 25 Petrie Plaza, Canberra City
Westpac – Petrie Plaza, Corner of Petrie Plaza and City Walk,
    Canberra City

Hospitals
The Canberra Hospital, Garran
Tel: (02) 6244 3394

If you are a victim of crime or need community advice:
Police Service
Weston Police Centre
Corner of Unwin Place and Streeton Drive, Weston, ACT
PO Box 401, Canberra City, ACT 2601
Tel: (02) 6256 7777
Tel: 131444 for non emergency
Tel: 000 Emergency

Cool places to hang out...
- Eat al fresco at the great cafe's and restaurants.
- Head for the centre of the city's nightlife in the Civic and Manuka districts.

Things to do in Canberra...
- Wander across the roof of Parliament House... honestly.
- Take the time to enjoy the awe-inspiring Australian War Memorial and the Anzac Parade.

TOWN BY TOWN

Tasmania

Tasmania is a truly unique place – and completely different to the rest of Oz. It's a region full of green hills and dramatic mountains – ideal if you're into trekking or climbing. The cities are also well worth a visit, and there's plenty to see and do. Hobart's slow atmosphere is deceptive, as it has a vibrant nightlife and presents plenty of opportunities for getting out and about and enjoying yourself.

Hobart

Why Hobart?

Good food, great art galleries and a surprisingly buzzing nightlife make little Hobart a hidden gem. Its quiet exterior hides a city that has a huge amount to offer any visitor, from great places to eat out to simply soaking up the beautiful buildings of Australia's second oldest city. You can also easily head out from Hobart to explore the rest of Tasmania, a stunningly unique place that you'll never forget.

SOME HOBART FACTS...
- ► Tasmania has officially the cleanest air in the world!
- ► Hobart is the second oldest city in Australia after Sydney.
- ► Hobart's Theatre Royal is the oldest in Australia.

Tasmania

INSET

King Island

LEGEND

Major Highway	unsealed
Main Road	unsealed
Minor Road	unsealed
National Highway Number	
Primary 'A' Route	
National Park / Reserve	
Conservation Area	
World Heritage Boundary	
Lake	

0 10 20 30 40 50 60 70 km

© Hema Maps Pty Ltd   Cartography : Ray Martin

N

BASS STRAIT

Banks Strait

FURNEAUX

Flinders Island

Cape Barren Island

Clarke Island

SOUTHERN OCEAN

TASMAN SEA

Smithton
Wynyard
BURNIE
DEVONPORT
Ulverstone
Penguin
Latrobe
Railton
Sheffield
Deloraine
Westbury
Mole Creek
Perth
Longford
Cressy
Evandale
LAUNCESTON
Scottsdale
Lilydale
Ringarooma
St Helens
St Marys
Stanley
George Town
Beaconsfield
Beauty Point

Savage River National Park
Arthur Pieman Con Area
Pieman River State Reserve
Rosebery
Zeehan
Queenstown
Strahan

Cradle Mountain
Lake St Clair
National Park
Walls of Jerusalem Nat Park

Great Western Tiers Conservation Area
Campbell Town
Ross
Swansea

Franklin-Gordon
Wild Rivers
National Park

Derwent Bridge
Bothwell
Hamilton
Oatlands
Triabunna

Southwest National Park

Mount Field Nat Park
Bridgewater
New Norfolk
Richmond
Sorell

HOBART
Huonville
Kingston
Geeveston
Dover
Southport

Freycinet Peninsula
Maria Island National Park

Tasman Peninsula
Forestier Peninsula

North Bruny Island
South Bruny Island
South Bruny National Park

Hartz Mtns Nat Park

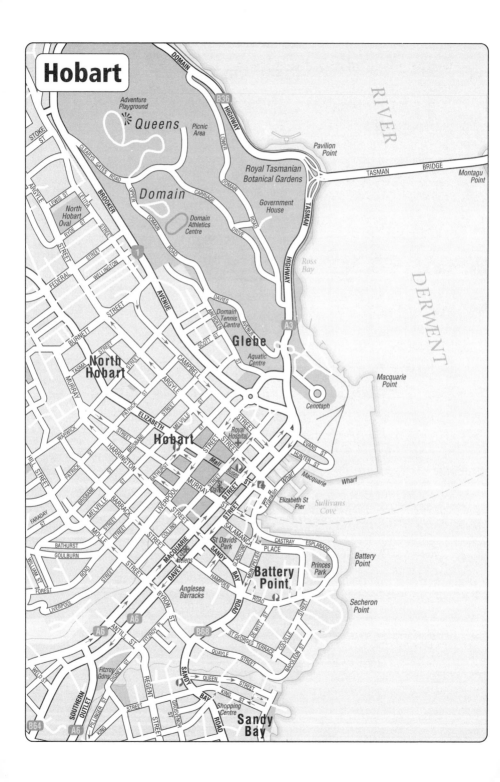

Getting to and around Hobart

Bus: Simply make your way to the Airporter bus at the front of the airport once you have collected your luggage, and tell the driver your accommodation destination. Airporter Shuttle Buses service the majority of Hobart's motels, hotels, backpackers and car rental outlets. Local passengers can be transferred to any bus terminal or taxi stand in Hobart City. And pleasantly, there's no need to make a reservation.

Taxi: The Taxi rank is located right outside the domestic terminal building.

Accommodation

Rentals
L.J. Hooker Hobart
1st Floor, 65 Murray Street
Tel: (03) 6234 4311
Fax: (03) 6234 4112
Email: *hobart@ljh.com.au*
Website: *www.ljhooker.com.au/hobart*

Raine and Horne - Hobart
175 Collins Street, Hobart TAS 7000
Tel: (03) 6231 0000
Email: *hobart@rh.com.au*
Website: *www.rh.com.au*

USEFUL INFO
► To call Hobart from the UK ring 0061 + 3 + eight digit number.

Hostels

Adelphi Court YHA 17 Stoke Street, New Town – (03) 6228 4829

Montgomery's Private Hotel & YHA Backpackers 9 Argyle Street, Hobart –
   (03) 6231 2660

AAA Old Hobart Centre Hotel Pty Ltd – 1300 766 406 (Backpackers
   Accommodation)

Map Adventure Bay Holiday Village – (03) 6293 1270

Allport's 432 Elizabeth Street, North Hobart – (03) 6231 5464

Budget Bunks 86 Argyle Street, Hobart – (03) 6234 6730

Map Central Cafe Bar 73 Collins Street – (03) 6234 4419

Central City Backpackers 138 Collins Street, Hobart – (03) 6224 2404
   or 1 800 811 507

Narrara Backpackers 88 Goulburn Street, Hobart – (03) 6231 3191

New Sydney Hotel and Backpacker Inn 87 Bathhurst Street, Hobart –
   (03) 6234 4516

Ocean Child Hotel 86 Argyle Street, Hobart – (03) 6234 6730

Work

Harvest work in Tasmania

Below are a few places where it's possible to get a job fruit picking
in Tasmania, along with all the best times to go and how far away
they are from the major cities. For a more expansive list, visit
www.jobsearch.gov.au/harvesttrail/ where jobs are listed and frequently
updated, and get information galore on each town.

TRAVEL TIP
▶ You'll be tempted to lie around in the sun all day, but you have to
be ultra-careful. Keep your skin out of the sun – use a hat, sun
block etc. and drink plenty of water. Apart from protecting you from
burning, it will help to stop you getting sunstroke.

Richmond

Richmond is just 27km to the north east of Hobart. There are many historic monuments here, with the most famous of the town's attractions being the Richmond Bridge over the Coal River, which was completed in 1825.

March to May – *grape picking*
June and July – *grape pruning*
November to January – *seed vegetable production*
December to April – *stone fruits including apricots, peaches, plums, cherries and apples*

New Norfolk

New Norfolk, which is around 40km away from Hobart, was home to many convicts from Norfolk Island who were shipped from New Norfolk during 1807-1808, and is now is one of biggest hop farming towns.

March and April – *hop picking*
March and April – *grape picking*
June and July – *grape pruning*
October – *stringing hops*
December and January – *cherries*

Office work

SKILLED – 1300 366 606
WORK & TRAINING LTD – 1300 309 675
COOPERS RECRUITMENT – (03) 6224 0574
ADECCO – (03) 6211 4400
AUSTRALIAN JOBSEARCH – 136268
JULIA ROSS RECRUITMENT – 1300 139 922
JOB NETWORK – 131715
MANPOWER – 132502
JET PERSONNEL & RECRUITMENT – (03) 6234 7966
A WAY WITH WORDS – (03) 6231 6559

ACCESS EMPLOYMENT – (03) 6234 8908
ADECCO (Employment Services) – 132993

Accountancy
HAYS – (03) 6234 9554
ADECCO – (03) 6211 4400

IT
DRAKE PERSONNEL – 131448
HAYS – (03) 6234 9554
ADECCO – (03) 6211 4400

Hospitality employers
Bars that may employ travellers on Working Holiday Makers (WHM) visas
Montgomery's Hobart Hotel 87 Argyle Street, Hobart – (03) 6234 4790
Cornish Mount Tavern 24 Barrach Street, Hobart – (03) 6234 5054
New Sydney Hotel 87 Bathurst Street, Hobart – (03) 6234 4516
The Astor Grill 157 Macquarie Street, Hobart – (03) 6234 3809
Bridie O'Reilly's 124 Davey Street, Hobart – (03) 6224 9494
Brooke Street Bar Sullivans Cove 19 Morrison Street, Hobart –
        (03) 6234 6254
Customs House Waterfront Hotel 1 Murray Street, Hobart –
        (03) 6234 6645
Globe Hotel 178 Davey Street, Hobart – (03) 6223 5800
Irish Murphy's 21 Salamanca Place, Hobart – (03) 6223 1119
Ocean Child Hotel 86 Argyle Street – (03) 6234 6730

Hobart hotels that may employ travellers on WHM visas
Hobart Mid City Hotel 96 Bathurst Street, Hobart – (03) 6234 6333
Oakford (Serviced Apartments) Australia Elizabeth Street Pier, Hobart-
        1800 620 462
The Old Woolstore Apartment Hotel 1 Macquarie Street, Hobart –
        1800 814 676

Montgomery's Private Hotel 9 Argyle Street, Hobart – (03) 6231 2660
Cambridge Hotel 860 Cambridge Road, Cambridge – (03) 6248 5010
AAA Old Hobart Centre Hotel Pty Ltd 67 Liverpool Street, Hobart –
   1300 766 406
Ascott International Hobart – 1800 620 462
Battery Point Guest House 7 McGregor Street, Battery Point
   (03) 6224 2111
Beachside Motel-Hotel 2 Beach Road, Kingston Beach – (03) 6229 6185
Black Buffalo Hotel 14 Federal Street, North Hobart – (03) 6234 7711
Irish Murphy's 21 Salamanca Place, Hobart – (03) 6223 1119
Isobar 11a Franklin Wharf, Hobart – (03) 6231 6600

Agencies
ADECCO – (03) 6211 4400
HAYS – (03) 6234 9554

Nursing
Agencies
DRAKE PERSONNEL – 131448
HAYS – (03) 6234 9554
ADECCO – (03) 6211 4400
OXLEY NURSING SERVICE PTY LTD – 1300 360 456
NURSELINE HEALTHCARE PERSONNEL – (03) 6224 6333

WORK TIP
▶ A copy of your CV can be saved on your email. This means you
can simply print it off when you need it, without getting it crumpled
up in your backpack. Take a smart outfit for interviews and work, or
you can always budget to buy a suit and some shoes while you're
travelling.

You will need to register as a nurse at:
Nursing Board of Tasmania
15 Princes Street, Sandy Bay TAS 7005
Tel: (03) 6224 3991
Fax: (03) 6224 3995
email: *NBT@nursingboardtas.com.au*

Teaching

A great place to start looking for jobs is to register with the Department of Education in Tasmania's E-Pool service at *http://epool.education.tas.gov.au*. It's the Tasmanian Department of Education Fixed Term and Relief Recruitment Register. You should also contact MANPOWER on (03) 6214 0270, who recruit relief teachers for the state.

For information on registering as a teacher :
Level 4, Kirksway House, 2 Kirksway Place, Battery Point, Hobart
TRB.admin@education.tas.gov.au
Tel: (03) 6233 5992

Support

Internet cafes
Drifters Internet Cafe, Shop 9, 33 Salamanca Place
Internet Central – Tas Access, Level 1, 29 Elizabeth Street

Hobart Information Centre
20 Davey Street, Hobart
Tel: (03) 6230 8233
Open Mon-Fri 8.30am-5.15pm; Sat-Sun 8am-4pm

Tasmanian Travel Centre
80 Elizabeth Street, Hobart, TAS 7000
Tel: (03) 0230 0250

Banks
ANZ – 40 Elizabeth Street, Hobart
Westpac – 28 Elizabeth Street, Hobart

Hospitals
Royal Hobart Hospital, 48 Liverpool Street
Tel: (03) 6222 8308

If you are a victim of crime or need community advice:
Police Headquarters
43 Liverpool Street, Hobart TAS 7000
Tel: (03) 6230 2375
Tel: 131444 to contact nearest police station
Tel: 000 Emergency

Cool places to hang out...
- Salamanca Place, Sullivan's Cove, North Hobart and Sandy Bay all have great bars and restaurants.

Things to do in Hobart...
- Shop till you drop at Salamanca Market.
- Hang out in some of the great pubs and bars downtown – Battery Point and Salamanca Place are popular hotspots.
- Head for the Cadbury's factory for a 'tasting'.

4 Web Directory

Working in Australia

General work
www.abs.gov.au
www.gwendalyne.com
www.jobsearch.gov.au
www.mycareer.com.au
www.seek.com.au

Harvesting
www.anyworkanywhere.com
www.goharvest.com
www.jobsearch.com.au
www.payaway.co.uk
www.wwoof.com.au

Hospitality & tourism
www.wagenet.gov.au
www.artisan-recruitment.com
www.hospo.com
www.spectrum-international.
    com

Hotels
www.hilton.com
www.langhamhotels.com
www.novotel.com
www.rydges.com

Internships
www.ccusa.com
www.globalchoices.co.uk
www.internships.com.au
www.ispc.com.au

Nursing
www.alliancehealth.com.au
www.anmc.org.au
www.gordon-nurses.com.au
www.healthstaffrecruitment.com
www.nursingagency.com.au
www.nursexel.com.au
www.nurseworldwide.com.au
www.OBSHealth.com
www.oxleynursing.com.au
www.qnc.qld.gov.au
www.wana.com.au

Office work
www.exact.com.au
www.hallis.com.au
www.hays.com.au/job/index.
    aspx
www.intgroup.com.au
www.jobsearch.gov.au
www.kellyservices.com.au
www.kpmg.com.au
www.manpower.com.au
www.momentumconsulting.
    com.au
www.robertwalters.com
www.tempsonline.com.au
www.ultimateaims.com

Ski work
www.bunac.org
www.ski.com.au
www.skiingaustralia.org.au

Sponsoring agencies

www.bunac.org
www.overseasworkingholidays.
  co.uk
www.councilexchanges.org
www.visitoz.org

Sporting gap years

www.flyingfishonline.com
www.sportlived.co.uk

Studying

www.australiangraduate.com
www.ozdegree.com
www.studiesinaustralia.com
www.studyaustralia.com.au
www.studyinaustralia.gov.au
www.studyoptions.com

Teaching

www.dest.gov.au
www.select-education.com.au
www.teacher.on.net

Visas

www.australia.org.uk
www.australianembassy.ie
www.immi.gov.au.
www.travellers.com.au
www.visafirst.com
www.workpermit.com

Volunteering

www.bunac.org.uk/uk/
  workaustralia
www.gap.org.uk
www.globaladventures.co.uk
www.govolunteer.com.au
www.i-to-i.com
www.voluntarywork.org
www.volunteerinternational.org
www.worktravelcompany.co.uk

Travel essentials

Accommodation
www.bakpakgroup.com
www.basebackpackers.com
www.hostelaustralia.com
www.hostelworld.com
www.nomads-backpackers.com
www.vipbackpackers.com

www.visitnsw.com.au
www.wakeup.com.au
www.yha.org.au

Communications
www.0044.co.uk
www.backpackersworld.com
www.blogger.com
www.cafesydney.net
www.card4anywhere.com
www.care2.com
www.cyberchat.com
www.fastmail.co.uk
www.globalgossip.com
www.iscard.com
www.itas.com.au
www.koalanet.com.au
www.msn.com
www.mytripjournal.com
www.myworldjournal.com
www.netstuff.com.au
www.orange.co.uk
www.sim4travel.com
www.t-mobile.co.uk
www.telstra.com.au
www.theoutlook.com.au
www.three.co.uk
www.travelblog.org
www.travelpost.com
www.travelvault.com
www.vodafone.co.uk
www.whitepages.com.au
www.yellowpages.com.au

Emergencies
www.fco.gov.uk/
   knowbeforeyougo
www.hic.gov.au
http://bhc.britaus.net

Flights
www.ebookers.co.uk
www.impulse.com.au
www.lastminute.com
www.opodo.co.uk
www.qantas.com.au
www.statravel.co.uk
www.virginblue.com.au

Gay and lesbian
www.galta.com.au
www.gayaustraliaguide.bigstep.
   com

Insurance
www.acetravelinsurance.com
www.duinsure.com
www.navigatortravel.co.uk

Money
www.oanda.com
www.xe.com

Tourist Information
www.australia.com

Transport

www.autopiatours.com.au
www.contiki.com
www.greyhound.com.au
www.gsr.com.au
www.ozexperience.com
www.railpage.org.au
www.travellers-autobarn.com
www.westrail.wa.gov.au
www.wcr.com.au

Travel guides

www.gapwork.com

Travel safety

www.fco.gov.uk/travel

Weather

www.bom.gov.au
www.bbc.co.uk/weather/
   world/australasia

Useful local websites

www.google.co.au
www.smh.com.au
www.theaustralian.com.au

City by City

Adelaide
General

www.adelaidecitytourist.com
www.adelaide.southaustralia.
   com
www.touradelaide.com

Hostels

www.adelaidebackpackers.com.
   au
www.bluegalah.com.au
www.cannonst.com.au
www.eastparklodge.com.au
www.sunnys.com.au

Hotels

www.hoteladelaide.com.au
www.hotelrichmond.com.au
www.majestichotels.com.au

Alice Springs
General

www.alicesprings.nt.gov.au

Bars

www.boslivesaloon.com.au

Hostels

www.alicelodge.com.au
www.anniesplace.com.au
www.desertroseinn.com.au

www.melanka.com.au
www.toddys.com.au

Barossa Valley
General
www.barossa-region.org

Hostels
www.tanundacaravan-
touristpark.com.au
www.parks-sa.com.au

Employment Agencies
www.creamcareers.com.au
www.rowanrecruitment.com.au
www.jobsearch.gov.au/

Brisbane
General
www.ourbrisbane.com

Hostels
www.bananabenders.com
www.hostelbrisbane.com
www.palacebackpackers.com.
au

Hotels
www.carltoncrest-brisbane.
com.au
www.couran-cove.com.au
www.mirvac.com.au

Bunbury
Hostels
www.adelaidebackpackers.
com.au
www.bluegalah.com.au
www.cannonst.com.au
www.eastparklodge.com.au
www.sunnys.com.au

Hotels
www.hoteladelaide.com.au
www.hotelrichmond.com.au
www.majestichotels.com.au

Byron Bay
General
www.byronbayonline.com.au
www.byronbaynow.com
www.visitbyronbay.com

Bars
www.byronbaynow.com/
nightlife.html

Hostels
www.aquarius-backpack.
com.au
www.artsfactory.com.au
www.byron-bay.com/
backpackersinn
www.byronbay-bunkhouse.
com.au

WEB DIRECTORY

work and travel in
australia

BUNAC'S *Work Australia* programme offers gap year students the chance to work and travel for up to 12 months in Australia. With the Working Holiday Maker Visa, you can take casual work to top up your finances as you travel around this amazing country. Visiting Sydney, Ayers Rock, Perth, Queensland and the Great Barrier Reef is all part of the experience.

Work Australia offers:

- Round-the-world flight ticket with extended validity

- Group flights and organised stopovers in Hong Kong, Bangkok or Vancouver

- Exciting choice of return routes

- In-country support services.

For more information or to download an Application Form, please visit the BUNAC website.

020 7251 3472 www.bunac.org

Dept. GP1, BUNAC, 16 Bowling Green Lane, London, EC1R 0QH E-mail: downunder@bunac.org.uk

Cairns
General
www.tnq.org.au

Hostels
www.carvella.com.au
www.dreamtimetravel.com.au
www.tropicdays.com.au
www.travoasis.com.au

Canberra
General
www.canberratourism.com.au

Hostels
www.canberrabackpackers.
   com.au
www.citywalkhotel.com
www.hostelcanberra.com

Darwin
General
www.arounddarwin.com.au
www.nttc.com.au
www.streetsofdarwin.com.au
www.whatsondarwin.com

Hostels
www.anniesplace.com.au
www.elkesbackpackers.com.au
www.banyanviewlodge.com.au

Hotels
www.botanicgardens.com.au
www.darwincentral.com.au
www.mirambeena.com.au

Geelong
General
www.geelonginfo.com
www.intown.com.au

Hostels
www.hostelmelbourne.com

Gold Coast
General
www.australia-goldcoast.
   com.au
www.goldcoasttourism.com.au
www.hellogoldcoast.com.au

Hostels
www.aquariusbackpackers.com
www.hostelbrisbane.com
www.surfersparadiseback-
   packers.com

Hotels
www.gci.com.au
www.marriott.co.au

Hobart
General
www.discovertasmania.com.au

Melbourne

General

www.ngv.vic.gov.au
www.vicartscentre.com.au
www.visitmelbourne.com
www.visitvictoria.com

Bars

www.melbournepubs.com

Hotels

www.flindersbackpackers.
   com.au
www.hostelmelbourne.com

Perth

General

www.inperth.com.au
www.streetsofperth.com.au

Hostels

www.beattylodge.com.au
www.coolibahlodge.com.au
www.hostelperth.com
www.murrayst.com
www.old-firestation.net
www.undergroundback-
   packers.com.au

Hotels

www.burswood.com.au

www.greenwoodhotel.com.au

Sydney

General

www.bluemountainstourism.
org.au

www.bridgeclimb.com.au

www.cityofsydney.nsw.gov.au

www.foxstudios.com.au

www.sydneyoperahouse.com

www.sydney.com.au

www.sydneyaquarium.com.au

www.timeout.com

www.zoo.nsw.gov.au

Bars

www.sydneycafes.com.au/
bars.html

Hostels

www.aegeancoogee.com.au

www.bondibackpackers.com.au

www.funkhouse.com.au

www.hostelsydney.com

www.originalbackpackers.
com.au

www.surfsidebackpackers.
com.au

www.wanderersonkent.com.au

www.wizardofoz.com.au

Hotels

www.civichotel.com.au

www.stamford.com.au

www.starcity.com.au

www.starwoodcareer.com

TRAVEL TIP

▶ Find out as much as you can about a hostel before you book it, or use a reputable company like Hostelworld or VIP Backpackers – not all hostels are as safe as we would like them to be!

5 Traveller's Checklist

Traveller's checklist

There's loads to remember before you go away on your gap year, and in the excitement it's easy to forget things. That's why we've put together this checklist.

Please note – we're not saying that you have to take all of this, but the list should get you thinking about the things you need to take and the things you need to do before you go.

Don't use this list as a 'must have' list, but more of a 'I never would have thought of that' list. Also bear in mind airline baggage allowances. Most airlines will allow an absolute maximum of 32 kilograms for checked-in baggage and 6 kilograms for hand luggage. Anything over this and they'll charge you for the excess.

For the more obscure items, hardware stores and general stores usually have things like bathplugs tucked away somewhere. If in doubt, your parents will probably know somewhere where you pick them up.

Baggage

Rucksack
Day backpack
Shoulder bag
Rucksack liner
Stuff sack
Document wallet

Sleeping

Sleeping bag, liner, inflatable
    pillow or neck cushion
Self inflating sleeping mat
    and/or foam mat
Ground sheet/poncho
Mosquito net
Tent

Eating

Bowl
Cup
Mess Tins
Knife/fork/spoon

Cooker
Bottle

Essentials

Maps
Guide books
Cord
Compass
Electric adaptor
Sew kit and strong thread
Safety pins
Calculator
Pocket dictionary
Note book & pen
Transparent wallets
Ear plugs
Books
Alarm clock
Watch
Washing line
Bathplug
Playing cards/games
Pritt stick

TRAVEL TIP
▶ Buy a phonecard and call home from a payphone. Check out some of these sites for more info: *www.card4anywhere.com*, *www.iscard.com*

Security

Money belt
Padlock
Chain

Light/Fire

Torch
Lighter
Matches
Candle

Water

Water bottle
Water purification tablets

Clothing

Long sleeve shirt x 2
T shirt x 2
Sweatshirt
Socks x 3
Dress/skirt/sarong

Waterproofs/poncho
Track suit bottoms
Fleece
Thermals
Trousers x 2
Shorts
Swimwear
Underwear x 3
Boots (walking)
Sandals/flip flops/jellies
Hat
Large cotton scarf
Smart clothes for job interviews

Hygiene

Travel towel
Shower towel
Toilet paper/tissue
Condoms
Sanitary protection
Soap
Soap box
Shower gel
Toothpaste and foldup
    toothbrush
Laundry soap

WORK TIP
▶ Be smart, upbeat and clean and tidy when you go for an interview
– you'll have a lot of competition!

Shampoo
Hairbrush/comb
Razor and shaving cream
Wash bag

Health

Immunization (including
  certificates)
Sun screen
Insect repellents (DEET)
Insect killer (Permethrin)
Medical first aid kit
Vitamins
Malarial tablets
Moisturizing lotion

Documents

Passport
Visas
Money/cash/dollars
Vaccination certificates

Passport photographs
Photocopies of all documents
Document Pouch
Air/travel tickets
Drivers licence
Travellers cheques
Credit card
Travel insurance

Other

Batteries
Camera
Sunglasses
Swimming goggles
MP3 player
Film
Binoculars

TRAVEL TIP
► Going online is probably the easiest and most convenient way to keep in contact with those you've left behind. You can find internet cafes all over Australia, and their rates are mostly very cheap. So get typing! You could also try the numerous online photo albums and travel blogs that are out there, like *www.mytripjournal.com*.

Index

INDEX